Discovering Language with Children

Discovering Language with Children

Edited by

Gay Su Pinnell
Ohio State Department of Education

National Council of Teachers of English
1111 Kenyon Road, Urbana, Illinois, 61801

NCTE Editorial Board: Paul Bryant, Thomas Creswell, C. Kermeen Fristrom, Rudine Sims, Robert Hogan, *ex officio*, Paul O'Dea, *ex officio*

Associate Editors: Marguerite Bougere, Carol Fisher, Doris Gunderson

Consultant Reader: Carlton M. Singleton

Book Design: Tom Kovacs

NCTE Stock Number 12102

Library of Congress Cataloging in Publication Data

Main entry under title:

Discovering language with children.

    Collection of articles prepared by the NCTE Committee on Language Acquisition of Young Children.
    Includes bibliographies.
    1. Children—Language—Addresses, essays, lectures.
2. Language arts (Preschool)—Addresses, essays, lectures.   3. Language arts (Elementary)—Addresses, essays, lectures.   4. Language acquisition—Addresses, essays, lectures.   I. Pinnell, Gay Su.   II. National Council of Teachers of English.   Committee on Language Acquisition of Young Children.
LB1139.L3D55   372.6   80-24795
ISBN 0-8141-1210-2

Contents

III. Evaluation in Language Education

Preface

The current highly productive period of research in the language acquisition of children coincides with a turbulent and confused period in the teaching of language arts. Furor over declining test scores, cries for the development of so-called diagnostic skills in teachers, and demands for accountability, particularly in the teaching of reading and writing, culminate in a back-to-the-basics movement aimed at the development of literacy. Commercial publishers and educators, often unaware of recent research in language learning, produce programs and materials designed to assure the public that schools are indeed teaching the basics. It seems difficult to make connections between research findings, classroom practice, and what educators tell parents about how their children become literate.

The time is right to take a new look at the role of language in the total development of the child. Much research is available and scholars are excited about new developments in linguistics and psychology and their implications for education. Adults who directly affect and are concerned with children as they grow and learn need to be able to make sound instructional decisions and to be able to say why they made those decisions. Teachers are ready to improve their knowledge and skills—not so much by engaging in additional remedial efforts or by identifying learning disabilities or deficiencies—but by increasing their understanding of how children learn to talk, read, and write. This collection of articles, prepared by the National Council of Teachers of English, Committee on Language Acquisition of Young Children, addresses those needs.

At its formation, the Committee on Language Acquisition of Young Children was charged with the task of examining research on the language acquisition of children and finding ways of making that knowledge available to people who work directly with children. Specifically, the purpose of the Committee was described in the following statement from the NCTE *Directory*.

Function: This committee will seek to develop materials for a
bulletin which will be addressed to practitioners in the community of language teachers—professionals, paraprofessionals, and
parents—who have roles in children's language acquisition.

In line with its stated purposes, the Committee began to develop
plans for a publication which would present a variety of issues
regarding language acquisition and relate them to current concerns
of teachers, parents, paraprofessionals, and others in the school
community. Committee members made a number of initial decisions concerning the publication.

The publication would present a collection of original articles
by recognized scholars in the field of language acquisition
and development.

Articles would be based on current research and would attempt to present findings and implications in a direct, readable form.

Each article would present a brief look at a single aspect of
language arts research and teaching.

Articles would utilize examples and illustrations and wherever
possible would present concrete implications for classroom
practice.

Articles would be directed toward building the understandings essential for effective classroom practice in the language
arts.

Selected references would guide readers to further study.

Subsequent to outlining a theoretical framework for the volume,
Committee members identified needed articles and solicited manu-
scripts. Written materials were reviewed by Committee members
and were also read and evaluated by a sample of teachers, parents,
and others who work directly with children. The resultant publication attempts to present information that was once the exclusive
domain of linguists and psychologists, in a way that will provide
practitioners with a foundation for instructional strategies.

Reporting on research findings often requires a specialized
vocabulary which sometimes creates barriers between researchers
and those who might use their findings—in this instance, those
who work directly with children. In this publication, an effort
has been made to avoid those barriers. Where precise vocabulary

is necessary, definitions, examples, and elaborations provide clarification.

The collection of articles in *Discovering Language with Children* is organized into three interrelated sections. Section One, "Language and the Young Language Learner," focuses on what and how children learn as they begin to acquire their language. The topic of language differences is also explored. In Section Two, "Language Growth in Educational Environments," articles center on creating in the school environment a context that will foster the further language development of children. Some articles focus on the beginnings of reading and writing in the very young child; others present implications for language arts education—speaking, reading, writing—applicable to the full range of students in the elementary school. The final section, "Evaluation in Language Education," deals with techniques and issues related to accountability in the language arts and points to new directions in the search for information about how children learn and develop language.

It is hoped that these original articles will make current research accessible to those who may be interested in language learning but have little time to perform an extensive literature search. While the articles cover a wide range of selected research in child language acquisition and development, the Committee made no attempt to treat the whole scope of language acquisition research or of teaching in the language arts. The collection serves as an introduction and overview for readers.

The articles are based on a number of assumptions about how children learn and use language. Language learning is emphasized as a process of discovery; it is rooted in action. It is created in the family and the culture, and developed through interaction with others in the environment as people use language for a variety of social functions. As children learn language, they learn to pay attention to what others intend to mean and to communicate meaning to others. Learning language, then, means learning concomitantly a system for making meanings and another for sharing meanings. Children learn the structure and patterns of their language; they also learn a system of social uses. They learn to maintain interest in conversation, to initiate, to take turns, to respond appropriately, to anticipate a conversational partner, and to distinguish between what is unknown and what is shared by the other. Children come to school with a language they have learned as part of their lives. When they enter the school environment, they should find supporting culture for their language development—one that helps them to expand knowledge and grow in skill while feeling confidence in and appreciation for what they have already learned.

Gay Su Pinnell

I Language and the Young Language Learner

Marguerite Bougere, editor
Tulane University

Part One: Starting with the Child

To plan effectively for language education, we must first think carefully about the nature of language and how young children learn it. We can begin by examining what children bring to the school situation—that is, knowledge and ways of acquiring it. The articles in Part One focus on language learning as an active process. Children hear language all around them. They make hypotheses about language structure and use. Through using language for a variety of their own purposes, they become increasingly skillful at communicating meaning. Language is developed and extended through the whole range of experiences and interactions in which the child engages.

Menyuk's article, "What Young Children Know about Language," stresses the active nature of language development and the "hypothesis testing" behavior that young children exhibit. Language development is described as a process of discovering rules and patterns rather than merely an imitation of adult speech. In the next article, Hood explores the special role that imitation does play, particularly in the development of interactional skills. Beaven describes "just play" activities, common to childhood, which have significance for the development of language and thinking skills. Finally, Zutell examines the significant differences between the way children learn language at home and at school and makes suggestions for assisting children as they make that transition.

What Young Children Know about Language

Paula Menyuk
Boston University

Children are active in developing their language by translating what they perceive about the language they hear and then testing those linguistic "hypotheses," gradually approximating adult usage.

Providing opportunities for children to interact with an adult, to use language and get a response, is essential for further growth.

By the time most children enter school they are communicating very effectively with others in their environment. This means that over a period of five years the child has learned a great deal about both the structural rules (grammar) of language and how to use language appropriately to convey needs, feelings, and thoughts. The rapidity of this development is even more astonishing when one observes that word usage begins at approximately one year of age, and by age three some children are producing complex and conjoined sentences, such as "Are there frogs swimming in there?"; "I want the red crayon and the green crayon."; or "My aunt, she live on Washington street, gave me a birfday present."

How does the child accomplish this seemingly formidable task during the preschool years? And, how can we use the child's knowledge of language at home and in school to enhance further development?

There is substantial evidence to indicate that language development is an active, not a passive, process. From birth, the child is engaged in testing hypotheses about the structure and use of language. Children do not merely imitate what they hear. Early sound-making and later imitation of utterances are modifications that reflect the child's level of understanding of the structure of the language. In a sense, children translate what they perceive into speech productions and then they test those productions. What appear to be errors (that is, differences between adult speech

5

and the child's speech) are in fact stages in the child's development of knowledge of the language.

For example, while gaining knowledge of negative forms of utterances during a particular developmental period, a child may perceive the difference between "he did not go" and "he didn't go." The child may translate "he didn't go," producing "he no go," but at the same time be able to *judge* which is the correct form when given examples of both forms. The apparent errors really reflect what the child *knows* about language during a given period of development.

Children perceive forms and test them by matching their own productions and those of others against those perceptions. By testing their productions they come to their own conclusions about how well the forms serve their purposes. That process is called *hypothesis testing*. As children mature, both perception and production of forms in the language systematically change. At first a child may perceive only that negative utterances contain a "no" or "not." As the child's perceptions change, so will the corresponding productions change. The child will produce, over time, such utterances as "no go," "he no go," "he no do go," "he don't go," and finally, "he didn't go." Such changes show that the child is perceiving new forms and developing new ways to produce them. When we refer to language learning as an active process, we mean the child's ability to form these new hypotheses and test them. The hypothesis testing abilities of the child account for the rapid development of language that takes place over the first five years of life.

The examples above also serve to illustrate that language development cannot be based merely on imitation of adult speech models. Productions such as "he no go" or "feets" or "camed" represent generalizations of the rules children have learned. They are trying to apply those rules to the speech they produce. The child does not hear adults produce generalizations such as "runned" or "he no go." They are a product of the active process of hypothesis testing.

Communicative interaction between the child and others in the environment is an important factor in fostering language development. Recent studies have indicated that adults who care for children are usually sensitive to the child's level of language development and attempt to make their language understandable to the child. They do not tend to correct the structure of the child's utterances. Rather, they give attention to what the child is trying to communicate, to the meaning of the utterance. Adults in the home are generally willing to accept and interpret the child's utterances to keep the conversation going, thus encouraging the communicative interaction that provides opportunities for the child to test the structures of language.

The way in which children go about acquiring language can be enhanced or depressed by school experiences. Several factors may play a role in whether language development will proceed smoothly once children enter school. Since they must develop their own hypotheses about the structures of language based on what they hear and the response they get when speaking, it may be difficult for them to understand why certain common utterances are unacceptable to a teacher. For example, the child who hears parents and friends saying "ain't" may be surprised at the teacher's disapproval. Children need to learn that there are different ways of saying the same thing, and they can do this by analyzing language and becoming more aware of its different uses. Telling children that what they say is wrong, or even having them repeat the different form, will not encourage analysis or awareness. It will only create insecurity about using language.

Our knowledge of language comes from our own experiences in using it, not from grammar books. We do not process the sentence "The boy hit the ball" by telling ourselves that it has a subject and predicate and is composed of an article + noun + verb + article + noun. We do not tell ourselves that the sentence "The boy who wore a hat" is wrong because the main sentence has no predicate. We have intuitive knowledge of the role of words in sentences and the relationships expressed in utterances. We know what "sounds right" to us. At an early age, children share much of this intuitive knowledge. If we allow the child to exercise those intuitions by making judgments about utterances, we encourage analysis of language in a way that knowing the names of parts of sentences does not.

Finally, a rich variety of opportunities for communicative interaction in the classroom will provide the language material from which the hypotheses develop. If most of the communication comes from the adult in the classroom, particularly if talk is primarily composed of questions such as "Did you finish the paper?", the opportunities will not occur. Children need to engage in interaction with a variety of people and in a variety of situations. They need to use language in many different ways and to hear varying kinds of language.

Children are intuitive grammarians. If they were not, they would be unable to reach the state of language knowledge evidenced on entrance to school. Our attitudes toward children's use of language, the ways in which we teach them about language, and the opportunities we provide for language use can either help or hinder the further development of language knowledge.

References

Brown, Roger. *A First Language.* Cambridge, Mass.: Harvard University Press, 1973.

Menyuk, Paula. *Language and Maturation.* Cambridge, Mass.: M.I.T. Press, 1977.

Menyuk, Paula. "That's the 'same,' 'another,' 'funny,' 'awful' way of saying it." *Journal of Education* 158 (1976): 25–38.

The Role of Imitation in Children's Language Learning

Lois Hood
Empire State College, SUNY

Children construct language for themselves rather than directly imitating adult speech; however, imitation plays a special role in language acquisition.

Children imitate for a variety of purposes, particularly to relate new information to things they already know.

Do all children imitate speech? If so, what kind of speech? And when and how do they imitate? For a long time imitation simply was not a topic of interest to researchers in child language acquisition. The reason for the omission went something like this:

> Obviously it is impossible for children to imitate everything they hear.
>
> It is also impossible that everything children say is something that they have previously heard.
>
> Therefore, imitation is of no importance in the language acquisition process.

In other words, if imitation can't account for everything, then it doesn't count for anything. We have come a long way from that point of view and consequently have discovered many fascinating things about imitation and its role in language learning.

For example, we now know that children differ in the amount and content of what they imitate. Some children imitate a lot; other children hardly at all. Both ways are common and entirely normal. The naturalness of both and the contrast between them can be seen in these examples of two children, taken from a recent study.

Peter: 21 months

Observations	Adult	Child
Peter opens cover of tape recorder.	Did you open that?	open/open/open
Peter watches the tape recorder.		open it
	Did you open the tape recorder?	tape recorder

Allison: 19 months

Observations	Adult	Child
Allison jumps up, almost hitting her head on an overhead microphone (the microphones had been adjusted by the cameraman before video filming began). Allison touches the microphone. She turns to Mommy.		man
	Man. That's the microphone.	
Allison points to another microphone on her mother's neck.		mommy
	Yeah. Mommy has a microphone.	
Allison looks at overhead microphone.	That's another microphone.	
Allison, still looking at overhead microphone.		man

We don't know the conditions that caused Peter to imitate the speech he heard and Allison not to imitate it, but the examples lead us to some notions about the kinds of words and structures that children imitate (if they imitate) and the conditions under which they imitate. We can also speculate about the functions which imitation serves.

In general, children imitate what they are in the process of learning; things that are at either extreme of their repertoire are not usually imitated. So, entirely new words are not likely to be imitated by a child, unless they are embedded in a familiar context, say a common kind of sentence or a common situation. Similarly, very familiar words or sentences tend not to be imitated, with the exception of routines such as games and stories. This notion of the importance of the relationship between new information whch is being acquired and old information which is presumably known is a crucial concept, not only for early language learning, but for later language learning and many other aspects of development throughout life. This concept has been a guiding principle of some of the most influential theorists in developmental psychology, notably Piaget and Vigotsky.

Why Do Children Imitate?

Examinations of what and how much children imitate tell only part of the story. Other important questions concern who they imitate, and the kinds of activities and settings of which imitation is a part. Researchers are just beginning to study imitation of language from the perspective of its communicative function. And we're finding out some surprising things about imitation's role in the development of conversational skills.

For instance, young children seem to repeat part of what their mothers say as one of the earliest ways to stay on the topic. Although very young children observe "turn-taking" rules of conversation with others, the infant and adult are not "talking" about the same thing. These are conversations in form, not in content. One of the first ways that children use to continue an ongoing topic is to repeat part of what has already been said. For example, in describing what might happen upon opening and setting up a doll house, I said (about a friend who was present), "She might pinch her fingers." The two-year-old with whom we were playing said, "pinch her fingers." Young children playing with each other (with no adult around) have also been observed to use imitation as a major tool of turn-taking.

This strategy of using what has already been said to stay in the conversation doesn't just disappear from the child's repertoire as the child learns more about language. Rather, it becomes embedded in other uses of language. Instead of merely repeating what someone else says, the child at a later point will repeat and then add new information about the same topic. For example,

Adult: I see two buses.

Child: I see two bus come there.

This illustrates one important point about how language develops. Specific strategies and language structures are incorporated into other strategies and structures to enable language use of greater complexity.

Perspectives in Language Acquisition Research

The questions of what language children imitate, and how much and why have been examined in light of current language acquisition research which emphasizes the interactional nature of the language learning environment. In studying the special role of imitation and of language learning in general, three points should be emphasized:

1. Language develops in rich contexts of interaction and communication;
2. Language meaning, use, and structure develop together and should be studied together; and
3. Part of development consists of certain linguistic skills becoming transformed and embedded in others.

In part, these three points represent a major perspective in language acquisition research today. They can apply equally well to educational issues relating to later language learning and should figure in our planning and evaluations of curricula.

References

Bloom, L., and Lahey, M. *Language Development and Language Disorders.* New York: Wiley and Sons, 1978.

Dale, P. *Language Development.* 2d ed. New York: Holt, Rinehart and Winston, 1976.

Learning through Inquiry, Discovery, and Play

Mary Beaven
Fairleigh Dickinson University

Activities we consider to be just play—building things; participating in art, music, and movement; and dramatic and sociodramatic play—are important in developing both language and thinking skills.

Participating in these so-called projective activities is a necessary part of learning to use the symbols and mental images of abstract thinking.

As young children play and pretend, they develop their language and form inner representations of their world. Activities such as construction, music, art, movement, drama, and sociodramatic play are often called projective, because into them children project their impressions of the world. They form and reformulate their inner representations as they observe and recognize discrepancies between their surroundings and their own view of them. When they discover something new in the world, they incorporate the new impressions into their play. They redo, rebuild, recreate, replay, and retalk to assimilate their discoveries.

Apparently, extensive participation in such projective activities is necessary for children to develop the ability to manipulate symbols and images mentally, an ability necessary for reading. Between the ages of five and seven children gradually internalize the projective activities. They report that they are able to play and talk "in their heads." Because the academic work of the school depends upon this internalization, children are not ready for formal instruction until they can talk and play in their heads. Adults must help children develop their thought and language abilities through construction, creative expression, and play which in turn will help them to separate the name of the object from the object itself.

Construction

Blocks and other building materials serve to translate mental images into concrete representations. Although much construction occurs through chance, children do use their impressions of their world to guide building activity. At times youngsters become frustrated because they lack the physical skills to make what they build look like their mental picture of it. But the discrepancy between what they produce and what they have in mind motivates them to continue building. At the same time, they continue to modify their images as they construct.

Children need a variety of building materials, space, and time—as well as contact with adults—to expand their concepts, language, and problem-solving abilities. Adults help by observing what children are constructing and then by creating a variation so that youngsters note the discrepancy and figure out how to make it. Adults also pose questions, such as "What does that look like?", "What could we use it for?", "What else do we need?", or "What would happen if you put this piece over here?". As important as this adult interaction is, children also need to work by themselves, without other children or adults. In this time alone, they incorporate what they have heard and seen, test their own ideas, and construct new forms.

Creative Expression

Just as blocks and other building materials serve as a means of translating mental images into concrete representations, so do drawing, painting, clay modeling, music, and movement activities. Through such creative activities, children expand, organize, and clarify their perceptual impressions and related language. Since children do not absorb all the sensory aspects in one exposure and do not organize all their impressions in one attempt, many creative experiences are necessary. Adults can help children perceive discrepancies between their representation of them and the actuality: "The dog you modeled has four legs, and so does that dog over there. Do you see anything else about the real dog that you want to add?"

Different media foster different components of thought. Drawing and painting develop perceptual sensitivity to color and line and act as a means of organizing them; clay and other plastic materials help children organize line and space; dance and movement capture time and space; and music records sound through time. The more media children use to organize their perceptions and concepts, the greater the complexity those concepts and the related language will have.

Dramatic and Sociodramatic Play

Dramatic and sociodramatic play provides practice in the use of symbols when language abilities are developing. Dramatic play emerges when children are two or three years old. They see adults using objects, and then they imitate them. Through their use of objects children try out their impressions of adult behavior. For example, one morning Ayan, the two-year-old son of a jazz trumpeter, woke his household, trying to blow his father's horn, dragging it on the floor, and announcing, "Me Daddy." He used an object as a symbol to represent his father; through the symbol he became Daddy.

Sociodramatic play emerges between the ages of four and seven. Dramatic play becomes sociodramatic play when several children play together on a theme, interacting both physically and verbally. As they play house, have tea parties, go on rocket trips, shop, or go to the doctor's, they add new information and change the play when needed. In replaying scenes, children reproduce their impressions of adult behavior and speech. Thus they refine their own language and mental representations of the world.

Play helps to move the child from concrete to abstract thinking. At first children use replicas of things adults use. Gradually they become less dependent upon such props and are able to use more undefined objects. During the period of sociodramatic play, children acquire the verbal and conceptual maturity to use verbal descriptions and miming gestures in place of objects. As they become more advanced in sociodramatic play, children plan who is to play what role, where the play will occur, what props are needed, and what problems they will handle. Planning may become so involved, intense, and satisfying that the children never actually play out their ideas. They no longer need overt action and direct physical participation, but can deal with it in words.

Apparently, talk alone is not enough to help children organize their concepts and develop their language. They need a structuring activity such as building, creative art and movement, or dramatic play into which they can cast their impressions of the world. A wide variety of studies indicates that one-to-one adult-child play interactions, story-telling, and field trips, followed by thematic sociodramatic play, and sociodramatic play using the manipulation of objects, are all good ways to foster growth of language and thought in children.

Teachers who want to promote maximum conceptual and language development will have their young students engage in projective activities that help children organize the nonverbal and verbal elements of their concepts. Construction, art, music, and movement activities, as well as dramatic and sociodramatic play, foster comprehensive development and prime the mind for the kinds of tasks found in the school.

References

Garvey, Catherine. *Play*. Cambridge, Mass.: Harvard University Press, 1977.

Engstrom, Georgianna, ed. *Play: The Child Strives Toward Self-Realization*. Washington, D.C.: NAEYC, 1971.

Sutton-Smith, Brian, and Sutton-Smith, Shirley. *How to Play with Your Children (and when not to)*. New York: Hawthorn Books, 1974.

Learning Language at Home and at School

Jerry Zutell
Ohio State University

There are essential, qualitative differences in how children learn language at home and how they are taught at school.

Teachers who know the significant aspects of each experience can help young children make the transition between home and school language learning.

During the first few years of formal education, young children must make a critical adjustment in the way in which they learn. They leave the secure environment of the family and begin to communicate in the broader social contexts of the school. With its more formal instructional modes, school is a new socializing influence on children.

Both the style and content of learning in school are different from home. When children use language at home, they can rely on familiar surroundings and parents whose activities and characteristic forms of expression supply substantial support for their verbal communication. In contrast, the school setting requires that children "play to a larger audience" and be more explicit in using language. Those demands are particularly significant in written language because writers cannot utilize nonverbal cues (pointing, or changing the pitch or volume of the voice) or receive immediate feedback from their readers (a nod, a quizzical look, or an "un-huh" of agreement) that would reveal the success of the communication.

When children start to school they are eager to learn and confident that they will make sense of the experiences awaiting them. And justifiably so! They have already demonstrated their learning ability through their mastery of the structures and systems governing their native language. Yet these same children who have already accomplished so much sometimes have great difficulty in mastering what would seem to be a natural continuation of communicative competencies—the ability to read and write effectively.

One source of children's problems with written communication may be the failure of the educational system to utilize both the language that has been learned and the *way* in which it was learned, in order to foster their further language development. An examination of the major contrasts between learning at home and at school may provide some insights as to how teachers can help children make the transition from one language learning environment to another.

Learning Language at Home

In the home, language learning takes place within the context of familiar surroundings and activities. Children use their natural curiosity as they shake, push, rattle, and bite the objects around them. Others interact with them, commenting, comforting, or even scolding. This action and accompanying talk provides nonverbal and verbal information in a meaningful context which children use to construct the rules governing language use.

Another characteristic of language learning at home is that it is a self-motivated, active, generative process. Parents do not consciously force children to talk by setting time aside each day to teach them sounds or by lecturing them on the seriousness and urgency of learning to talk. In spite of this, children are able to construct complex and sophisticated rule systems based upon the unstructured language information available to them. The process of learning language is not passive imitation; children actively create their own ways of expressing their ideas and observations. My son Justin's use, at sixteen months, of "Bye-bye bath!" as he watched the water draining from the tub was typical of the highly inventive, yet rule-oriented language created by all children.

An essential quality of learning at home is that children learn language by observing and doing. Smith (1975) has distinguished three modes of learning: performance (learning to swim by getting into the water and trying), demonstration (watching someone else swim), and verbal instruction (being told how to swim). At home children rely on the first two modes, speaking and listening to others speak, rather than waiting to be told how to construct sentences.

Early language learning is directly related to use (tacit) rather than being based on stated rules (explicit). We all apply highly complex rules in speaking. Even though we may be unable to state what those rules are, we know them tacitly. In contrast to school, the focus at home is on meaning, not structure. Parents don't tell the child who says "Mommy cookie" that there is no verb in that sentence. Using language to express ideas is the focus of language learning at home, and parents interpret their children's utterances as complete and meaningful even if they are ungrammatical by adult standards. Parents even modify their own language intuitively to fit their children's linguistic needs as they see them, using simpler sentences, different vocabulary, clarifying devices, and various attentional devices.

Learning Language at School

The language and the teaching materials at school often assume that all children have the same background, interests, and language knowledge. Children are expected to adjust to the experiences, language patterns, and focus of the learning tasks in their classroom.

As they learn language at home, children themselves organize and sequence information and skills. No one teaches them verb endings in a predetermined sequence before plurals or possessives. But in school, most programs and textbooks control learning by imposing a structure—typically a sequence of individual skills which are explicitly taught and systematically reinforced. Our language programs are organized around the scope and sequence charts that accompany basal texts, and we provide a weekly spelling list for children to learn according to our view of learning and organizational patterns.

The predominant modes of language learning at home are demonstration and performance; at school, oral instruction and skill practice take their place. Smith (1975) estimates that in the average hour of reading instruction, children spend only four minutes actually reading. Many activities are paper-and-pencil oriented rather than centered on making and doing things.

Parents tend to respond to the child's meaning and rejoice in each indication of progress. The role of the teacher is generally different: There is a strong demand for correctness, and teachers tend to view errors as failures rather than partial successes. The responsibility for effective communication and for progress falls upon children. Those who do not succeed may be labeled as being lazy, slow, or even disabled. The teacher's responsibility is too often viewed as controlling the context and motivation for learning, offering oral instructions or explaining the information in the texts, and monitoring progress and reporting it to parents.

Making the Transition

The above comparisons between home and school emphasize the extremes of each environment. Few parents provide the supportive conditions described here all the time; many teachers exhibit attitudes and techniques usually seen in parents. Further, as children grow in intellectual ability and knowledge base, parents as well as teachers begin to incorporate more directive and explicit techniques. Nevertheless, it is clear that the two language environments are significantly different, and often it is the difference in environment rather than a deficiency in the child that impedes success in school. Given the specific differences between the typical patterns of language development in home and school, there are some guidelines that teachers may follow to help children make the transition from one to the other.

First, if the children's backgrounds of experience are very different from that assumed by school texts or activities, begin by using the children's own experiences and then broaden their background. In reading, this might involve starting with language experience stories while regularly reading a variety of books and poems to develop their background further.

Next, there should be ample time for performance as well as oral explanation or instruction. The opportunity to read a book or make up a story or improvise a scene should not be a reward for those who finish their work early, but an essential part of every child's language arts program. Children need to use language on their own besides listening to their teacher's explanations or instruction.

Instead of starting with rules and generalizations, children need to begin with what they already know. Explicit knowledge of things such as phonics rules or correct spelling should be built on the tacit uses that have already been acquired. Giving children choices and presenting them with problems to solve, material to organize, and time to figure things out for themselves may be more effective than trying to preorganize their learning experiences.

Teachers need to emphasize content and communication rather than form. There should be opportunities for children to revise and correct themselves or be corrected without fear of failure. A genuine and supportive "I don't quite understand," or "Let's try it again," is much more effective than "No, that's not right. Next . . .". Teachers, like parents, who look for what is right very often find it, and those who look for errors or mistakes likewise find them. And children who are successful at the beginning are more willing to take on the lifelong task of learning.

References

Cazden, C. *Child Language and Education.* New York: Holt, Rinehart and Winston, 1972.

Farb, P. *Word Play.* New York: Bantam Books, 1973.

Smith, F. *Comprehension and Learning.* New York: Holt, Rinehart and Winston, 1975.

Part Two: Learning about Language Variety

Language has endless variety. People throughout the world speak many different languages, and there are numerous dialects or varieties of the same language. Most of us can give examples of the ways in which people in different locations talk differently. We also realize that people talk differently depending on their purposes for talking, those they are talking to, or the social situations they are in. Part Two of this section addresses those differences and what they mean for language learning. Language differences are viewed as differences, not deficiencies; variety is a characteristic of language, not a problem. Learning to vary one's own language and to recognize language variation in oneself and others is part of language learning.

In the first article, Jaggar focuses on helping educators understand dialect variation and adapt curriculum to meet the special and varied needs of language users. Language itself can be a valid topic for student examination. Dillon explores the dynamic and changing nature of language and describes how children can become collectors and surveyors of language variation and change. Teachers often encounter in the classroom children whose primary language is other than English. Urzúa presents information from recent research in second language acquisition, emphasizing the particular strategies used in acquiring a second language—recognizing that children who do not speak English are not so-called problem children, and placing such children in situations that have meaning for them.

Allowing for Language Differences

Angela Jaggar
New York University

Children whose dialects differ from standard English often encounter problems in school which stem from misconceptions about their language.

To help all children become effective language users, we need to understand dialect variation, be alert to the specific differences in children's language, and adapt curriculum to meet their needs.

Imagine two five year olds talking about their pets. One child says, "My dog runs fast," and the other responds, "My dog, he run faster." Both children learned English, but they don't speak it the same way because their cultural and linguistic backgrounds are different. Many American children learn some form of standard English, but many others come to school speaking so-called nonstandard dialects.

Recent research shows there is no reason to believe that nonstandard language in itself is a barrier to learning and communication. Nevertheless, because of widely held misconceptions about dialects, and popular but mistaken ideas about what is "good" and "poor" English, children who speak nonstandard English often encounter problems in school. If we are going to help children become effective users of language, we must understand that variation in language is natural.

We all speak a dialect! Bostonians do not sound like New Yorkers or Chicagoans. University professors do not talk like construction workers, at least not usually. To say a person speaks a dialect is to say only that he or she speaks a regional or social variety of English that differs from other varieties of the language.

All dialects are highly structured, complex languages. Standard English is no more logical, no more expressive, and no more communicative than nonstandard English. The meaning is the same, whether a child says "I ain't got no pencil" or "I don't have a pencil." Judgments about the superiority of one dialect over another are social judgments, not linguistic ones. If we understand this, we won't underestimate the language abilities of children who speak nonstandard dialects.

From a linguistic point of view, there are relatively few differences between standard and nonstandard English. However, teachers need to know what differences exist in their students' speech in order to avoid or modify instructional techniques and materials that may be confusing. These variations may appear in the vocabulary, pronunciation, or grammatical forms that children use.

Most variations occur in pronunciation. For example, nonstandard speakers may not pronounce the *r* and *l* sounds and the consonant clusters at the ends of words. As a result, words like *sore* and *saw*, *tool* and *too*, and *wind* and *win* sound the same. Other words that may be contrasted in standard English, such as *tin* and *ten*, *chair* and *cheer*, *right* and *rat* have identical pronunciations in some nonstandard dialects. The pronunciation rules thus produce different homonyms in children's language, just as *their* and *there* and *pail* and *pale* do in standard English. These and other differences are shared by many regional standard dialects and should not interfere with communication. The context should be sufficient to reveal the child's meaning, as in "Da *chair* cos' ten dollar."

There are fewer dialectical differences in grammar than in pronunciation, but these differences are the more stigmatizing. Speakers of standard English find them harder to accept and usually base judgments about the adequacy of children's language on the grammatical features in their speech. Unfortunately, teachers and others tend to interpret these differences as mistakes or errors when they are not. Dialectical variations are systematic and rule-governed, and children who produce nonstandard forms are following the rules of their language system.

Moreover, if we examine the grammatical variations we find they are relatively minor, surface, differences in language—for example, the absence of inflectional endings that mark possession, number, and tense, as in "She go every day," or "that girl house," or verb forms such as "He be tired," and double negatives like "Nobody can't find it." The sentence structure remains essentially the same. This is important! For it means that the differences between nonstandard and standard English are primarily differences in usage, not grammar. Not even the youngest speakers of nonstandard English will say "Ain't going he school to" for "He isn't going to school." But they may say "He ain't goin' to school" which is an equivalent form and means the same thing.

The differences in language have some obvious implications for teachers of children who use nonstandard English. Pronunciation differences present potential problems when children are learning to read, especially during phonics instruction. For example, rhyming lessons may become confusing if teachers do not realize that words that rhyme in their own dialect do not rhyme in the children's dialect and vice versa. Similarly, problems may arise in spelling if teachers are insensitive to differences in pronunciation. But just as speakers of standard English learn to write *idea* and *which* even though they say *idear* and *witch*, those who speak nonstandard English can learn to write *with* for *wif* and *ask* for *axe*.

Likewise, the grammatical differences should not interfere in the teaching of reading if we remember that in oral reading the goal is comprehension and not accuracy. When asked to read aloud, a child may convert a sentence like "He doesn't want anything" into "He don't want nuffin." These are not reading "errors" and need not be corrected. The change shows that the child has comprehended the written message and merely "translated" it into a more natural speech pattern. No child talks exactly as the books are written! Children who speak a more nearly standard English learn to read from texts written in language that varies, often considerably, from their own. So can children who speak nonstandard dialects. They already understand a more nearly standard spoken English and can learn to read, and write, it, even if they don't speak it themselves.

The crucial issue with regard to dialect differences is not a linguistic one. The major problem lies in our attitudes and knowledge about language in general and our attitudes toward dialects specifically.

We must recognize that there is no one "correct" way of speaking. What is right or proper for one speaker or situation may be wrong or improper for another speaker or situation. Attempts to erase language differences by correcting so-called errors or to teach standard usage patterns through rules of grammar and language drills not only are ineffective but often have undesirable consequences. Children who say "We ain't got none" and are told "That's not right. You don't have any" are bound to be perplexed. The teacher's response is meaningless because young children cannot separate form from content in language.

Our primary goal is to increase children's communicative competence—that is, the ability to use language effectively in a variety of situations and for different purposes. This is best accomplished by involving children in language activities that are meaningful and developmentally appropriate. Story-telling, role-playing, asking questions, sharing, and discussion are good examples. These "real" experiences, unlike language drills, encourage flexibility, fluency, and power in oral expression. As children learn how to communicate effectively, they develop an intuitive knowledge of how language varies in different contexts and they begin to master new language forms, including standard usage, in a natural way.

Our job, then, is not to change children's language but to help them expand the language they already have. We must start by accepting the children's dialects and recognizing that, though they are different, they are not deficient. Children can think logically, learn effectively, and talk intelligently in any dialect.

References

Burling, Robbins. *English in Black and White.* New York: Holt, Rinehart and Winston, 1973.

Williams, Frederick; Hopper, Robert; and Natalicio, Diana S. *The Sounds of Children.* Englewood Cliffs, N. J.: Prentice-Hall, 1977.

Teaching about Language Itself

David Dillon
University of Alberta

Variations in language are natural because language is dynamic
and constantly changes to meet different needs of its speakers.

Language has many appropriate forms that vary from one place
to another and from one situation to another.

For quite some time language arts programs have been focused on
teaching children about language by teaching grammar. This study
of the structure of sentences and labeling parts of speech has been
narrow in focus and very time-consuming. Such an analytical
study of language should be only a small part of the total language
arts program because it contributes in only a minor way toward
our ultimate goal of increasing children's ability to use language
effectively in speaking and writing. Only a great deal of purposeful
language use will accomplish that goal. Nevertheless, some knowledge about language itself is important for children to develop
appropriate attitudes toward language use. That knowledge must
be broader than the study of grammar and more reflective of the
basic nature of language as a social and communicative tool.

The Nature of Language

A brief description of a fourth-grader, Susan, getting ready for
school one morning, can indicate the kinds of language she encounters. Susan's grandmother, who lives with them, tells Susan
that her lunch is in the ice box. Susan is in a hurry as she gets it,
and her mother calls after her, "Susan, close the refrigerator door."
As she stops to do this, Susan hears the morning weather report.
It's an interview of a New England resident and sounds something
like "The stawm dumped a lawt of snow heah," and she wishes her
own Midwestern town would get some snow soon. She meets her
friends on the way to school and greets them one by one. "Hey,

what's up?" "Boy, sure is cold!" "Think it'll snow?" As they
approach the school, the children meet the principal. "Good
morning, Mr. Lawrence," Susan says. "How are you today?" He
responds and heads for his office as Susan and her friends hurry
to class.

This small slice of Susan's life illustrates two basic concepts
about language that both teachers and their students should
understand.

Language is dynamic, ever-changing over time. Susan's encounter with different terms, *ice box* and *refrigerator*, for the same
object from speakers of two different generations illustrates this
principle. Reading Shakespeare or perhaps glancing at a page of
Chaucer or Beowulf in the original makes it clear to us that our
language has indeed changed dramatically over time and continues
to do so. Of course we do not often see such sweeping changes,
but, like Susan, we occasionally see new words like *input* enter the
language while old ones like *fountain pen* slowly die.

In most cases, language changes over time in order to adapt to
new social needs. The Norman invasion of Britain left the English
language a little more like French. The expansion of the American
West brought a number of native American and Spanish terms into
American English. The technological explosion of the sixties and
environmental concerns in the seventies have left us numerous new
technological and ecological terms such as *ecodice.*

*Language has many appropriate forms that vary according to
place or social situation.* The differences in a society as diverse as
ours are reflected in the various forms of our language. Susan's
Midwestern ears noted some pronunciation differences in the New
Englander's dialect, although she probably didn't realize that she
would sound as different to the New Englander as he did to her,
or that she herself even spoke a dialect. Besides varying in pronunciation, regional dialects also differ in vocabulary: *creek, bayou,* or
stream; milk shake or *frappe;* and *poor boy, hoagie, submarine,
hero,* or *grinder.* A little later in the morning, Susan's informal
and formal greetings of "Hey, what's up?" and "Good morning,
Mr. Lawrence" indicated her awareness of language adaptation to
different social situations. We all use these social variations as we
move from casual to more formal settings or from speech to writing (for example, the informal "Jeet jet?" and the more formal
"Have you eaten yet?"). Whether we choose to use *cheap* or *inex-
pensive,* "I can't hardly wait" or "I'm anxiously waiting" or "I
shall await your response" may depend on many elements of the

social context and on whether the communication is spoken or written.

Several notions related to this principle deserve mention here. First, so-called standard usage is simply that language variety in any geographic region which we tend to use for more formal situations such as business or government. Some social groups may use language that is very similar to the standard variety at home; some groups may use a substantially different variety at home or with friends. Standard usage is appropriate for the formal settings, just as what we sometimes call nonstandard usage is appropriate in other social settings. Second, since each variety of a language serves its users equally well, there are no differences in quality or value among the regional or social forms. We can describe them as different from each other, not as superior or inferior to each other.

Instructional Implications

Our most natural and effective way to teach is inductive, starting from a number of known specifics or examples and leading learners on to make their own generalizations. Children can become collectors and surveyors of language variation and change.

Like Susan, children encounter examples of social variation in language at early ages as they hear relatives and family friends speak differently to various other people in certain situations. They themselves change their own language when "playing house" or "playing school." Television provides them with examples of language change, and teachers can add to this with films, recordings, and children's literature. Members of the community representing various social segments of the population can come to the classroom, or children can go out to the community to meet them, preferably as part of a larger project, perhaps in social studies.

To learn more about regional variation, students can have oral pen pals in different parts of the country by using cassette tapes. Such an exchange allows each class to learn about the distinctive aspects of their own language which reflect their regional heritage.

Historical change in language is also encountered in the home when parents or older relatives use antiquated terms such as *ice box* or *trolley*. These same family members are also the best source of data for classroom learning about words that have either died (*knickers* or *sock hop*) or been born (*skyscraper* or *videotape*) or changed (*crackerjack* to *cool* to *right on*) during this century. Students can survey relatives and friends for this information. A good way to begin a study of currently used words or phrases is to ask children if they have ever wondered about the origins of some of our idiomatic expressions such as "letting the cat out of the bag" or "pulling your leg." Students can choose their own examples to research. Along with their study of history, they can find examples of words that entered our language from other languages (*moccasin* and *skunk* from native American languages or *patio* and *rodeo* from Spanish).

Finally, we must remember that our goal is for children to acquire some generalizations about language. Which specific examples of social, regional, or historical variation we use to help them reach those conclusions is unimportant. The examples should arise from our students' backgrounds and interests and be sufficient in number for them to generalize. Then the chances are good that children will conclude that language variation is natural and reasonable; that these variations are all appropriate for a particular time and place; and that there are no inherent differences in value among them.

References

Gott, Evelyn, and McDavid, R.I. *Our Changing Language.* New York: McGraw-Hill, 1965 (record).

Joos, Martin. *The Five Clocks.* New York: Harcourt Brace Jovanovich, 1961.

McDavid, R.I., and Muri, J.T. *Americans Speaking.* Urbana, Ill.: National Council of Teachers of English, 1967 (record and pamphlet).

Shuy, Roger. *Discovering American Dialects.* Urbana, Ill.: National Council of Teachers of English, 1967.

Doing What Comes Naturally: Recent Research in Second Langage Acquisition

Carole Urzúa
Educational Consultant

When people learn languages they use many similar acquisition strategies; this is true whether they are small children learning their first (or native) language or older children or adults learning a second language.

Second-language learners go through several stages as they acquire their new language.

First- or second-language learning can only take place when and if the learner is placed in a situation that has meaning for that individual.

A recent cartoon illustrates a familiar experience: A pair of adult tourists, standing in a Mexican street, are observing two tiny children talking to each other. The man comments in amazement to his partner, "How can something so small conjugate irregular Spanish verbs without stopping to think?"

Everyone who has ever tried to learn a foreign language surely identifies with that question! Children seem to learn languages effortlessly, while adults labor to say even the simplest phrase; throughout the world, children with even a minimum of intelligence can learn their first or native language, but everyone (even a genius) has varied success in learning a second language.

What accounts for this difference? And, more important, what is it that helps all learners to learn a second language? For thousands of children in the United States, the answers to these questions are crucial to their success in school settings. Many children from Hispanic, French, Asian, and Native American backgrounds have been acquiring a native language at home which is sometimes different from that used by teachers in their schools. For such children, learning a second language efficiently and commendably is an important task. Thus their teachers, and other significant adults in their lives, need to learn all they can about what happens in the language-learning process so they can aid that process to the greatest extent. Parents, too, may wish to be well informed in recent language research. For example, many parents in Culver City, California, and in Canada have recognized the intellectual and social advantages of being bilingual, and have started their children in foreign language immersion programs, in Spanish and French, respectively.

Two aspects of second-language acquisition will be the focus of this paper: (1) Recent research in second-language acquisition (of both children and adults) shows that the processes used in learning a second language are very similar to the processes young children use when learning their first language; and (2) the learning of a second language is less difficult if the learners are placed in situations that have meaning for them. To demonstrate how these two aspects work, I will describe some processes used by both first- and second-language learners and examine the stages in which these processes take place.

Stage One in Language Learning

Have you ever heard parents say (or perhaps you have said yourself) "My child spoke in complete sentences from the very beginning." Perhaps those so-called sentences sounded something like the following: "Daddy go there," or "Me eat allgone." There's no doubt that these sentences convey some meaning, but they are far from being complete, adult sentences. However, for one who is just beginning to learn a language (Stage One) it is important to grab at almost anything in order to open the door to communication. Sometimes nonverbal means suffice. Sometimes one word ("Lights?") works. Sometimes it is a group of words (called a *formula* by Wong-Fillmore, 1976), which are acquired and used as unanalyzed wholes in the situations in which they fit. It does not matter whether the words form a grammatical structure; at first, it is only important to let your friends know that you want to communicate with them, or as Wong-Fillmore says, to "lubricate conversational gears!" These formulas, when learned, seem to function in that way.

Several years ago I went to live in the Philippines as a Peace Corps Volunteer. Facing 4,000 of my new friends on the first morning in my town, I knew that I wanted to convey the attitude that I liked them and that I wanted to talk to them. Seizing on a formula I had learned from my new "mom," I told them hello in their own language! There was an instant murmur through the crowd, followed by a great round of applause. My formula worked; 4,000 people now knew we were going to be working together to learn one another's language.

Wong-Fillmore studied five young Mexican children who entered the public school system in the United States. She noticed that each child began using formulas similar to those of the other four. In fact, by early fall, formulas constituted between 53 and 100 percent of the children's language (questions, commands, greetings, politeness routines, getting the floor, changing the subject). At the end of the year, only one child, Nora, used very few formulas. The other children still relied to a great extent on formulas in specific situations which gave the impression that they spoke the language so the listener would be encouraged to perform a vital function—continuing the conversation!

Stage Two in Language Learning

For most learners of a second language (and a first), however, there is a strong motivation to communicate more than "Hello!" Most learners have ideas to share, feelings to express, jokes to tell. From the vast sea of language around them, they must extract certain elements of the language that they have figured out, to convey those ideas and feelings. Thus, learners move, after widely varying lengths of time, to Stage Two. Even here, however, not much of the structure of the language is available to them. They have only a few "drops" of language to analyze, because they cannot comprehend the whole "sea" at once. Since the formulas have already been learned, many learners change the formulas to invent new ways of expressing their ideas. Thus, the question formula "How do you do these?" for one Mexican child in Stage One became, in Stage Two, "How do you do these flower power?" and "How do you do these in English?"

Other strategies learners use in Stage Two (adults and children alike) are the same as in Stage One: they simplify the language structure, conveying the message in the chunks of meaningful words, and they take rules that they have inferred from some structures and apply them, even where they do not fit.

Simplification. Those who have learned more than one language (and are old enough to talk about it) remember simplifying a great deal. All verbs, for example, may have been reduced to their simplest form—perhaps the present tense. Thus, I communicated to my friends in my second language that "I teach—yesterday."

Or, commonly, children learning English as a second language will talk about their "two pencil" and "Rosa book." Such language is similar to that of a twenty-nine-month-old native English child who told her mother that "Mary give block me" when questioned about an alien block among the little girl's toys (Urzúa, 1977).

In fact, if learners did not simplify the grammatical structures to some degree, they could not talk. Leaving the details of the language (word endings, auxiliary verbs, and so on) until later, learners often choose words that convey the meaning and merely string them together.

Overgeneralization. Besides simplifying language structures, learners often understand a rule of grammar and use it too much; this strategy is called overgeneralization. The best example of this is the first- and second-language learner's development of past tense. As learners understand that "ed" on the end of certain words indicates talking about something that has already happened, they frequently say things like "jumped, licked, singed (a song), writed, hurted." The rule, then, for past tense is used in places where it does not fit—that is, on irregular verbs. Until there has been more exposure to the language and more practice in using past tense, that powerful rule (or generalization) will be used in all situations requiring a past tense. Commonly, children in kindergarten and first grade whose native language is English still overgeneralize past tense. Second-language learners may take several years to learn the irregular verbs.

If persons learning a second language are especially lucky in Stage Two, they will be talking to responsive, caring persons who recognize that making errors and taking risks is important. In fact, the better language learners are those willing to take risks (Omaggio, 1978). Researchers in second language acquisition are presently trying to describe sequences of development of certain structures. One such sequence might be: What ride in? What he ride in? What he can ride in? What can he ride in? Young children might use any of these sentences, and their parents would certainly not call them deviant or chide them for not using adult grammar. In fact, parents would be listening to the meaning of the message, and probably would make a response to that meaning, such as "What can he ride in? How about the wagon?" (Corder, 1974; Richards, 1974). Likewise if second-language learners are to use the powerful processes of learning available to them, they must be encouraged to be active in their communication efforts, trying things out, risking, and getting responses (feedback) from

persons around them who care about the message they are conveying. Using the considerable social skills available to her, the little
Mexican girl Nora, mentioned earlier, sought out English-speaking
children to engage in oral dramatic activities. By the end of two
and a half months, Nora no longer relied on Spanish at all. Count-
ing on her friends to respond to her communication efforts, and
talk back to her, Nora gained rapid facility in her new language.

Stage Three in Language Learning

Persons who want to become a part of the community by speaking
the new language will not stop at Stage Two. Often they desire to
master more grammatical devices and more nonverbal and cultural
nuances so they will be more precise and appropriate in their
communication. In this stage many children and adults alike ask
a lot of questions about their new language. For some, the analysis
of specific grammatical forms may be conscious as in reading or
grammatical exercises. For others, using the language more and
more will ultimately facilitate finer tuning of the language.

The time needed to reach this stage varies widely. Two of the
Mexican children in Wong-Fillmore's study had reached this stage
within one year, and one child had barely crossed that threshold.
Two children were very far from being aware of the means by
which they communicated their ideas and feelings. In a program
that I helped organize for the teaching of English as a second
language in the Honolulu, Hawaii, public schools, at the end of
one year very young (below age 6) immigrant children could
scarcely be differentiated from children whose native language
was English. Primary children usually took two years, and children
older than 11 took much longer to reach the level of mastery of
grammatical details.

Throughout all recent discussion of research in second language
acquisition, grammatical (linguistic), social, and cognitive strategies are seen as alternating, and compatible, processes for all
learners. For a learner to be free to learn another language, the
learner must be able to trust others to respond to the messages
communicated and not be laughed at or singled out. In addition,
a learner must be active in seeking people to talk with, and willing
to do what is necessary to conform to the standards of these
speakers. In taking risks and using whatever language is available,
learners (adults and children) will undoubtedly use many formulas
and simplified language forms, and will overgeneralize language

rules and constantly hypothesize about how to make the language work. And just as most people learn their first language by using these same acquisition processes, learners of a second language will be most successful if the speakers and listeners around them just do what comes naturally!

References

Corder, S.P. "The Significance of Learners' Errors." *New Frontiers in Second Language Learning.* Rowley, Mass.: Newbury House, 1974.

McLaughlin, B. *Second Language Acquisition in Childhood.* Hillsdale, N. J.: Laurence Erlbaum Associates, 1978.

Omaggio, A. "Successful Language Learners: What Do We Know About Them?" *ERIC/CLL News Bulletin* (May, 1978): 3.

Peal, E., and Lambert, W. "The Relation of Bilingualism to Intelligence." *Psychological Monographs* 76 (1962): 1–23.

Richards, J. "Error Analysis and Second Language Strategies." *New Frontiers in Second Language Learning.* Rowley, Mass.: Newbury House, 1974.

Urzúa, C. *A Sociolinguistic Analysis of the Requests of Mothers to their Two-Year-Old Daughters.* Unpublished dissertation, University of Texas at Austin, 1977.

Wong-Fillmore, L. *The Second Time Around: Cognitive and Social Strategies in Second Language Acquisition.* Unpublished dissertation, Stanford University, 1976.

II Language Growth in Educational Environments

Carol Fisher, editor
University of Georgia

Part One: Creating a Context for Language Growth

Language is embedded in culture. Children come to school with a language developed in their culture, and they should find there a supportive milieu for further expansion and development of language. The school environment should provide rich and varied language and opportunities for children to make connections between what they already know and the new understandings they are trying to develop. Concrete experiences, surrounded by meaningful talk and written language, will facilitate the development of reading comprehension and writing ability. While younger children should concentrate on meaning rather than form, it may be appropriate for older children to focus directly on language itself in order to become aware of the patterns of language structure and how they relate to the communication of meaning.

Articles in Part One attempt to describe elements in the school environment which can influence positive language development in a variety of ways and provide a foundation for specific instruction in reading and writing. Fox's article focuses on activities that support the processes through which children learn and develop language. Natarella advocates wide exploration of a variety of books and extension of literature through various follow-up activities. Stewig suggests particular school activities which can link the classroom to language in the outside world. Pointing out that children continue to develop language during the elementary school years, Chomsky explores ways of helping them become more aware of the patterns and structures of language. In the last article, Fisher offers suggestions for helping children become aware of language structure—an alternative to traditional grammar lessons.

Promoting Growth in Oral Language

Sharon E. Fox
The Ohio State University

Many different activities—reading aloud, dramatic play, discussing, painting, building, observing and comparing—are essential to promote development of children's oral language.

The process of development involves the input of rich and varied language, opportunity for children to hypothesize about how it works, test or practice new words and structures, and finally obtain feedback about their use of language.

During a visit to a first grade classroom I saw several boys wearing foil-wrapped boxes on their backs. "An oxygen tank?" I asked one. "No!" he quickly responded, "a life support system." This was worth watching, I thought, so I observed their play of going to the moon. Here is part of the dialogue I heard:

"Ready to go!" one yelled.

"Oh, no we're not!" said another. "We've got to test ourselves for dizziness and no gravity and see if we can run on the moon and do flips."

"Have to test out the parachutes!"

"No, no parachute," corrected one player, "cause if we parachute, we'll go up, not down."

They started on their journey after placing their imaginary spaceship on a higher course. The block corner across the room became their moon landing area.

I noticed one boy walking around with his arm dangling on one side. "What are you doing?" I asked. He said they were on the moon and he had hurt his arm. Later he told the others he needed a "bionic arm." They accepted his statement without questions.

Another group of children were making a rocket nearby. They joined the first group by saying, "Calling Spaceship Number One! Calling Spaceship Number One! We're sending up a small spaceship with some Martians in it for you to study." And the play continued.

These children were using language quite skillfully to assist their play. Imaginings needed to be verbalized in order to continue the sociodrama, for the participants had to understand and accept each other's role interpretation. As an example, the new group wishing to enter the play scene acknowledged the ongoing drama by speaking in "radio" language—"Calling Spaceship Number One!"—and linked themselves as contacts for Martian research.

The dialogue reflects the *input* of many experiences the youngsters had previously had. Television probably served as the main source. They may have seen reruns of *Star Trek*, Saturday morning children's shows such as "Space Academy," and "The Six Million Dollar Man," or perhaps news documentaries of actual rocket launchings. These children took in not only the ideas and information but also some of the vocabulary and usage. The initial exchange, "An oxygen tank?" "No, a life support system," illustrates the knowledge of specific vocabulary appropriate for space adventures as opposed to underwater explorations. In their play the children also exhibited procedural knowledge in regard to equipment (the parachutes) and a human's reaction to a new environment (doing flips).

The actual language used demonstrates the fact that children process only what they are able to understand at that time. They base hypotheses on those understandings. Some of the statements reflect a surface knowledge. True, scientific investigations are performed when space travel occurs, but sending Martians to the moon for study is a little far-fetched.

Play afforded these children an opportunity to reaffirm and *practice* prior learnings, to *test* new hypotheses on others. The *feedback* each child received provided additional information to be processed and a chance to expand and elaborate their interpretations. The players gave feedback in two ways: first by direct correction, as in my mislabelling the life support system and one child's blast-off announcement "Ready set go!" when no testing had occurred; and second, indirectly, as in the group's acceptance of an idea or language being used and a continuation of the play activity.

This procedure of input, hypothesis, test/practice, and feedback as evidenced in the previous dialogue is, quite simply, the way in which children acquire and refine language. All of the learning work occurs within a meaningful context—that is, youngsters hear and use language purposefully. Sometimes the situation is imaginary, as in play; at other times the situation involves the ongoing events of living.

Common experiences form a basis for talking. Study trips are especially useful because they include concrete, authentic experiences from which children can extend their vocabularies and continue their learning after returning to the classroom. Not all trips require outside transportation. Students who are studying architecture can take a walking tour of the homes and buildings in the area surrounding their school. Input of new vocabulary words might include *dentils, fish scale* design, or even *shingles.* Testing and practicing these new acquisitions might occur while a small group constructs a model of a building or puts up a bulletin board to share what they have seen. Feedback takes place within the group and from the teacher. Informational books on the topic provide a source for both input and feedback.

The literature program is another way in which the teacher creates common experiences for students. As language input, reading aloud to the class is an obvious choice. In addition to the daily whole group session, smaller groups and individuals should hear stories read aloud too. And storytelling, another literature input source, happens too rarely for the value it has in the classroom. Straight telling—that is, direct eye contact with no props—is probably the most difficult, but it has the advantage of establishing a special rapport between speaker and listener. Other modes of storytelling use flannel board, puppets, chalk talks, and pictures.

Merely listening to stories read or told is not enough to promote language growth. Children need to try out and practice the language they have heard. Some may retell the story through puppets, dramatic play, or a flannel board. Others may respond by planning and drawing a mural or diorama. By working together, children have an opportunity to test and receive feedback on the language used—language influenced and extended by literature.

Oral language may be developed through extensions of books that children read for themselves. Besides the previously mentioned story activities, small group discussions on one book or several books by the same author and joint projects to formulate games are two of the many kinds of oral outcomes. Sharing books with others through brief summaries, role playing, and book "sales," all create yet another avenue for broadening and testing language.

Structuring the classroom to include a variety of areas, such as art and science centers, stimulates different kinds of language. Rich, diverse materials in an art center help to produce rich, diverse language. Construction paper, paste, and crayons as the only resources can restrict not only art expression, but also the ongoing language. Cloth remnants, ribbons, wallpaper, and wrapping and tissue paper provide textures, designs, and colors that lead to interesting collages. A box of plastic and cardboard containers suggests models, and another dimension is added. As children propose, discuss, and select materials, they use language purposefully to work on their tasks.

The science center may be a source of comparative language, for example, by demonstrating the likenesses and differences between two plants, one grown in sunlight and the other in shade. Careful observations of the classroom guinea pig might evoke descriptive language involving weight, measure, and movement.

A block-building corner and housekeeping area encourage imaginary language through play. Games require the participants to agree upon the rules and follow a specified set of procedures. Sand and water containers suggest such a variety of activities that hypothesis testing is a natural outgrowth of their use: Will one bottle hold as much as another? How many items can be placed on the plastic boat before it sinks?

The classroom environment should not be static. A continual rearrangement must take place with each learning area receiving different and new items according to the teacher's curriculum planning. Not all objects need to be replaced, for the familiar can acquire broader, richer meanings when compared or used with a new object. And sometimes a teacher can elicit a change in thought and thus a change in language, through questioning or pointing out a certain item's properties. Written questions in a display or placed in a center may also channel the way in which children formulate and solve problems.

Scheduling a daily sharing period provides time for students to explain, describe, and respond to questions. This more formal activity is a fine opportunity for a child to practice using language to reach the interests of a large group, and for the group to offer feedback on the presentation. A good sharing session does not just happen. The language skills of clarity, preciseness, brevity, and questioning have to be learned by establishing procedures and providing the chance for positive comments and constructive criticism.

Children need a balanced participation in dramatic play, work in small and large groups, listening and responding to literature, and having concrete learning experiences both in and out of the classroom. Teachers can promote linguistic growth within these contexts through the kinds of language input they provide, by allowing time and structuring different occasions for using language (testing and practicing), and by offering opportunities for feedback.

Related Readings

Language Use and Acquisition, Theory into Practice, vol. 14, no. 5. Columbus, Ohio: The Ohio State University, 1975.

Rosen, Connie, and Rosen, Harold. *The Language of Primary School Children.* Baltimore, Md.: Penguin, 1973.

Wagner, Betty Jane. *Dorothy Heathcote: Drama as a Learning Medium.* Washington, D.C.: National Education Association, 1976.

Sharing Literature with the Young Child

Margaret Natarella
Columbia Public Schools, Missouri

Children's language can be extended by sharing books that contain a variety of sentence patterns and rich vocabulary.

Language development can be enhanced by extending the stories through various follow-up activities.

To help children know and appreciate literature, we need to see that they have enjoyable experiences with books at an early age. Pleasant encounters with books, spearheaded by a respected adult, convey the idea that reading is fun and an enjoyable and profitable use of one's leisure time. Young children also need to hold books and look through them at a leisurely pace. This gives them an opportunity to "read" the story from the illustrations and helps them learn book-related concepts such as front and back, right and left, and top and bottom. Encounters with books can be enchanced by participating in a variety of oral response activities.

Through literature, children are exposed to new vocabulary and sentence patterns. When they come to school their language patterns reflect the spoken language of the home environment. For some children, school and home vocabularies and language structures are radically different, causing considerable frustration in the new environment until they learn the school-related vocabulary which enables them to function adequately. To develop their language, children need constant exposure to the different words and sentence patterns found in literature, especially when reading experience is extended with follow-up activities.

Literature is an excellent language building resource, especially when the experience is extended by oral activities such as discussion and dramatization. Such programs significantly increase aspects of word knowledge, quality of vocabulary, and reading comprehension.

Authors of fine books for young children do not water down the vocabulary nor purposely select one-syllable words. They often use figurative language, repetition of phrases and sentences, and new or unusual words to make the text a literary accomplishment. Figurative language is effective in Byrd Baylor's *The Desert Is Theirs*, illustrated by Peter Parnall: "Spider People were there too. When the new world wobbled, they sewed earth and sky together. It's together still. . . ."

New or unusual words are found in *Python's Party* by Brian Wildsmith. In this picture book for young children the author uses *cunning, scuffled, dabbing,* and *wobbled* as the animals perform their tricks. Children understand the meaning of the words from context, and they can pantomine their understanding as they "wobble along on two melons" like the world-famous hyena.

Some books repeat phrases or sentences which children often enjoy saying too after hearing them read. In fact, they become more attentive while listening for the clue words. *Have You Seen My Mother?* by Anne Maley (illustrated by Yutaka Sugita) repeats "Have you seen my mother?" eight times during the story. No doubt the sentence will be heard over and over during the day.

Another kind of book that invites involvement is one that requires the listeners to answer specific questions or respond in some other way. Brian Wildsmith's *Puzzles* has a question on every page that can only be answered by carefully observing the illustrations; and nursery rhymes such as pat-a-cake bid the children to say the verses and participate in the hand movements.

As mentioned earlier, the language of books can be enhanced by activities that follow the reading. Many books inspire oral activities such as discussion, dramatization, role playing, puppetry, and story retelling. These activities extend the literary experience by encouraging children to use the language structures and the vocabulary from the story in meaningful contexts.

A real-life occurrence that all children cope with is learning to tie their shoes. Barbara Klimowicz's *When Shoes Eat Socks*, illustrated by Gloria Kamen, is excellent for follow-up discussion that teaches young readers that others have this same problem as well as other frustrations of growing up.

Using the new words and phrases or sentences occurs almost automatically when children dramatize or retell a story using a flannel board. *The Three Bears* and *The Three Pigs* are excellent stories for such activities because the children become involved with the recurring language patterns in both. The creative incorporation of new language is shown by a three-year-old "wolf" who responded to the pigs with, "Then I'll huff your house in! Huff! Huff!"

Particular stories suggest special follow-up activities, which add another dimension to the literature experience. Cooking, art, movement, and nature walks are exciting things to do after sharing stories that feature these activities. For instance, making and eating chicken soup with rice must be done after sharing Maurice Sendak's *Chicken Soup with Rice.* And how many of your children have tasted cranberry preserves, tapioca pudding, or rhubarb pie, the foods craved by the peacock in Diane Massie's *Dazzle.* Having a tasting party would give the children an opportunity to try some new foods and find and use the special words that describe their taste, texture, and consistency.

Many nursery rhymes and folk tales have food as an integral element of the story. The three bears went for a walk while the porridge was cooling. The queen of hearts made some tarts. Lorinda Bryan Cauley uses these tales and rhymes in her illustrated cookbook, *Pease-Porridge Hot.* Some recipes included in the book are: Peter Rabbit's Mr. McGregor's Garden Salad, The Little Old Woman's Catch-Me-If-You-Can Gingerbread Man, The Three Bears' Hot-and-Yummy Breakfast Porridge, and Little Miss Muffet's Curds and Whey with Fruit and Nuts. Reading the recipes, following the directions, and talking about everything that happens are all important aspects of reading-cooking experiences.

Painting would be especially appropriate after listening to *Sleep Out* by Carol Carrick or *Dawn* by Uri Shulevitz. Art activities enable children to experiment with colors and textures as they express their thoughts and feelings in a different medium. A variety of materials and freedom to experiment are essential in such creative responses.

Movement activities are suggested by many experiences with literature, such as Byrd Baylor's *Sometimes I Dance Mountains:* "Dancing is a way of talking too because a dance can say *anything.*" As an extension of books and poems, children can create movement that expresses the wind, rain, flowers, frogs, and grass. They can prance, wriggle, or jounce, using their entire bodies or particular body parts in their interpretations.

After reading *Once We Went on a Picnic* by Aileen Fisher (illustrated by Tony Chen) or *Secret Places* by D.J. Arneson, children become more aware of the endless variety of things in the environment. A walk may focus on nature sounds, leaf and bark patterns, small creatures, or the many different plants in the area. On these walks the children are listening, observing, and discussing as they learn many new words that describe the objects in the environment.

In summary, sharing books with children should be an enjoyable experience for parents and teachers. The children, in turn, benefit from these encounters with literature because reading, and the supporting activities, broaden their experience, develop vocabulary, and in general provide a rich environment for growth in language development.

References

Arneson, D.J. *Secret Places*, photographs by Peter Arnold. New York: Holt, Rinehart and Winston, 1971.

Baylor, Byrd. *The Desert Is Theirs*, illustrated by Peter Parnall. New York: Charles Scribner's Sons, 1975.

Baylor, Byrd. *Sometimes I Dance Mountains*, illustrated by Kenneth Longtemps. New York: Charles Scribner's Sons, 1973.

Carrick, Carol. *Sleep Out*, illustrated by Donald Carrick. New York: Seabury Press, 1972.

Cauley, Lorinda Bryan. *Pease Porridge Hot: A Mother Goose Cookbook*. New York: G.P. Putnam's and Sons, 1977.

Fisher, Aileen. *Once We Went on a Picnic*, illustrated by Tony Chen. Scranton, Pa.: Thomas Y. Crowell, Co., 1975.

Galdone, Paul. *The Three Bears*. New York: Seabury Press, 1972.

Galdone, Paul. *The Three Little Pigs*. New York: Seabury Press, 1970.

Klimowicz, Barbara. *When Shoes Eat Socks*, illustrated by Gloria Kamen. Nashville, Tenn.: Abingdon, 1971.

Maley, Anne. *Have You Seen My Mother?*, illustrated by Yutaka Sugita. Minneapolis: Carolrhoda Books, 1969.

Massie, Diane R. *Dazzle*. New York: Parents Magazine Press, 1969.

Sendak, Maurice. *Chicken Soup with Rice*. New York: Harper and Row, 1962.

Shulevitz, Uri. *Dawn*. New York: Farrar, Straus and Giroux, 1974.

Wildsmith, Brian. *Brian Wildsmith's Puzzles*. New York: Franklin Watts, 1971.

Wildsmith, Brian. *Python's Party*. New York: Franklin Watts, 1975.

Planning Environments to Promote Language Growth

John Warren Stewig
University of Wisconsin—Milwaukee

A rich, productive language environment in the school links the classroom to the world outside.

Children need contacts with other people, with the community, and with objects that stimulate language.

In planning the school language environment for children, a major task is to establish links to the world of language outside the classroom. School language learnings have immediate value in proportion to success in establishing such links. The isolation of the classroom can be reduced by providing contact with people, objects from the environment, and field excursions. The nature and complexity of such links to the outside will vary at different levels, but it is crucial that they occupy a central position in productive language environments whether for three-year-olds or middle school students.

People

Classroom visitors from the community—parents or other adults—help expand children's understanding of language and their fluency in using it. For example, a teacher might invite people to the classroom who speak a foreign language. Young children are intrigued to learn that not everyone calls that four-legged object we sit on a chair. One year a kindergarten class kept a chart of different words for chair. Drawing from parents who had a knowledge of a foreign language and from other adults who visited the class, the list grew to include *égua* (Akan language from Ghana), *silla* (Spanish), *stuhl* (German), *Kēsā* (Hebrew), *kszesło* (Polish), *la chaise* (French), and *scaun* (Romanian). With older children such classroom visitors could teach children to say or write their names, a phrase of greeting, or perhaps even a simple rhyme.

Other visitors could include speakers of other dialects. After children have discussed the differences in their ways of talking (assuming at least some have come from another area), it is time to invite speakers who can provide information on regional dialect differences or on dialect as related to age or generational differences.

Visitors to the classroom may also motivate children to use the language skills they have already acquired. Classroom visitors who explain their jobs, crafts, hobbies, or special interests, provide for extensive language learning. First, preparatory reading will supply needed background. Then the children use their language skills in dictating a letter of invitation. Prior to the visit the teacher helps children formulate questions to ask. Important language growth occurs as students grapple with their original questions and reshape them to communicate clearly. A review of listening skills completes the children's preparation for the visit. While the visitor is in the classroom, students use listening and oral language skills in the conversational exchange that takes place. Following the experience, it is helpful to have children dictate or write an account of what occurred. The concluding activity is a thank-you letter to the resource person.

Objects from the Environment

A second important component in linking the classroom with the world is a conscious use of objects or artifacts which stimulate language. These are of three kinds—language-stimulus, language-related, and language-reproducing objects.

Language-stimulus objects are brought into the classroom to develop a child's ability to use oral or written language in describing something. For example, the teacher might bring in a persimmon, pomegranate, or other unfamiliar fruit or vegetable, and ask the children to observe its shape, color, texture, weight, smell, and taste. As children search for just the right words in talking or writing about the experience, they are developing expressive language skills.

Language-related objects include media materials such as books. A study of the book could include a hornbook replica, an old children's book (easily found in antique shops), braille and talking books, a book that reads from back to front (Hebrew or Chinese), and a good-quality pop-up book. Other possibilites include a book in its hardback, paperback, filmstrip, film, and recorded versions, giving children the chance to use language to discuss the similarities or differences, and their preferences. Such activities develop skills in describing, comparing or contrasting, and evaluating.

Language-reproducing objects allow children to study the ways in which others use language. Adult uses of language can be enjoyed and studied by listening to tapes or records of authors reading their own words. Encourage children to describe their reactions to the author's speech. Older children can read along as they listen and report how the book was enhanced by the author's oral reading. Films or videotapes of authors and illustrators explaining their work are widely available and are good alternatives or supplements to having a local author or illustrator visit the school.

An interesting study is to find out how children in other places use language. Tape recordings can be exchanged with a classroom in a distant part of the country. The topic might be social studies, but whatever the topic, a helpful understanding of the rich diversity of American English develops as children listen to the tape. The fifth graders in central Indiana discover that not everyone pronounces *pin* and *pen* identically, as the fifth graders in central Massachusetts learn that some people say *car* with an /r/.

Field Excursions

The classroom is only one of the many environments in which children can increase their linguistic competencies. Every community offers a variety of language environments that can be utilized by conducting field excursions. New and different experiences, laden with vocabulary, challenge children to think, talk, and then dictate or write about their impressions. Ideally these trips need to include cultural experiences, such as visiting an artist's studio; professional experiences, such as visiting an architect's office; commercial experiences, such as visiting a small business; and industrial experiences, such as visiting a factory. Such field excursions not only enhance language growth as children meet new words in a meaningful context, but they also provide career education opportunities for the social studies program. As mentioned earlier, children also encounter this richness of language when a speaker visits the classroom. The main difference is that field excursions change the focus (Stewig, 1980).

Excursions into the community can also be made for social service purposes. One third grade teacher regularly takes her children to a retirement home where they read from books of their choice, thereby sharing the pleasures of literature with the residents. Even the least able reader finds a willing listener, and the interchanges between adult and child are meaningful to both.

If there are limitations on the number of field excursions possible, teachers may need to search for places to visit within walking distance of the school, or use technology to bring the community into the classroom. The Hansens (1972) have described at length how the telephone conference call can be used, as early as kindergarten, to establish a link between the community and the school. As children interview city officials, chat informally with a nursery owner, ask questions of a newspaper editor, or plan for their excursion to a bank, they expand their language skills and develop understandings of how language functions in daily life.

A major problem with too many language programs is that children escape from them with the belief that school language is unrelated to the real world. We can overcome this by incorporating experiences with a variety of people, artifacts, and field excursions in the school language environments that we design—environments that reflect the vitality of language in life.

References

Hansen, Harlan S., and Hansen, Ruth M. "The Speakerphone in the Elementary School," *Elementary English* 49 (December 1972): 1262–5.

Stewig, John Warren. *Read to Write: Using Children's Literature as a Springboard to Writing.* New York: Holt, Rinehart and Winston, 1980, 39–41.

Developing Facility with Language Structure

Carol Chomsky
Harvard University

Language development continues throughout the elementary school years as children become more adept at dealing with increasingly complex linguistic structures.

Reading books, listening to stories, and specific language awareness activities help older children develop facility with language.

Children of elementary school age are still actively engaged in acquiring their native language. Language development is much slower than during the preschool years and not as noticeable as in the earlier years, but studies show that it continues in much the same manner as with younger children.

School-age children continue to learn new constructions systematically on their own, using the language they hear around them. They are prepared to construct their own internal language system from inputs that come their way and they benefit from exposure to a rich and varied linguistic environment.

Children progress at surprisingly different rates. In recent linguistic testing that I did with children between the ages of six and ten, I found that knowledge of a series of complex language structures varied widely. Age was not the whole story. Although in general the older children were more advanced, there was enough variation so that some of the seven-year-olds, for example, were several stages ahead of other children of nine and a half or ten.

What was different about the children in the study who progressed quickly as compared to those who moved along more slowly? Interestingly enough, the children's independent reading appeared to be related to their linguistic stage. Those who were read to more, and who read more on their own were the ones who knew more of their language.

Apparently it doesn't matter whether children listen to a book read aloud or read it themselves. What is important is the exposure to the language of books. Written language tends to be more complex than speech, and children who read benefit from a range of linguistic inputs that are unavailable to the child who has no access to books.

Some children in our study reported no reading at all in the course of a week, and others reported a great deal. Our heaviest reader, an eight-year-old girl, reported reading, in one week, *Borrowers Aloft, Little White Horse, Find the Constellations, Myrtle Albertina's Secret, Helen Keller, Pinocchio, The Enormous Egg,* a Charlie Brown comic book, *Amelia Bedelia,* and a number of stories. This child was in our top linguistic stage. Quite a variety of levels for a second grader! In general, reading at many different levels was characteristic of our heavy readers.

This research suggests that the kind of exposure and input provided by the written language is beneficial to children's language development. It would be useful for teachers to read aloud to children regularly, and to encourage them to read widely on their own, for pleasure. Books as complicated as children are willing to tackle are a good idea. It's all right to miss some of what is in the book in the excitement of getting on with it, and to skip less interesting portions. We all read that way. Careful, analytic reading has its place, but free, pleasure reading brings important contacts with large amounts of literary language. For other suggestions, see *Reading Is Only the Tiger's Tail,* where ways to encourage classroom reading are engagingly described.

Language facility can be developed also through a more direct approach. I think that, starting in the upper elementary grades, it is effective to heighten children's awareness of language and their sensitivity to sentence structure and word meaning. Rather than teaching facts of grammar, I suggest providing ways for children to become aware of features of language that they know implicitly and use, but have never had reason to examine directly. What I recommend are linguistic consciousness-raising sessions.

Sentence composition is a good place to begin. Children can construct sentences under a variety of conditions that make the process more interesting. The result must be a grammatical sentence. This leads to some strange word combinations and arguments over what is and is not a sentence. The children must exercise judgment about grammar and acceptability in language, and consider the form of language explicitly. They have to concentrate on the sentence construction itself and ask themselves repeatedly: What can come next so that this will be a sentence?

One way to proceed is to use a game called Alphabeteasers,

described by Joseph Shipley in *Word Play*, an intriguing book of language games. In Alphabeteasers, you start with any letter of the alphabet, and compose a sentence in which each word in succession begins with the next letter of the alphabet. For example, if you begin with the letter *b* you might write: Baby cougars don't eat fireflies. Sentences can be of any length, but longer ones are more challenging and more fun. Some sentences produced by a group of fifth graders who tried it were: "Orville planted quite rapidly six tulips under very wet xylophones," and "A black cat died early Friday going home in Joe's kooky limousine." Some fourth grade productions were: "Sally tasted used vinegar." "Michael never owed people quarters." It's fun and it requires specific focus on the mechanics of sentence composition.

Another game for making sentences uses an array of words such as this:

asked	they	know	you	can't
you	why	don't	home	go
forgot	I	say	want	to
he	that	believe	they	know

To form a sentence, start at any box, and move one box at a time, always to a neighboring box. The resulting string of words must be a plausible sentence. The children's productions can become quite complicated. One fourth grader included this sentence in a long list: "They believe I forgot you asked why they know you can't go home." His teacher liked this one because of his use of subordinate clauses, which did not usually appear in his spontaneous written work.

Children enjoy making sentences that are unusual; they aren't satisfied with ordinary ones. One group of children working together on another array produced the sentence "Turtles don't you see." I picked this one out of their sentence list as being ungrammatical, not a sentence. "Oh, yes it is," they argued. Here was their proof: "You come into a room and see things on the table and you don't know what they are and you ask, 'What are they?' And somebody tells you, 'Turtles, don't you see?'" They won their point.

Analyzing sentence meaning is another useful activity for linguistic awareness. Here an interesting way to proceed is to collect riddles and analyze why they are funny. Children enjoy making their own riddle books and exchanging them with friends. The source of humor in many riddles is linguistic and there is much to be gained in language awareness from this analysis. For example, there may be an ambiguous word in the question: "Where was Solomon's temple? On the side of his head." Or the ambiguous word may be in the answer: "Why is a barn so noisy? Because all the cows have horns." Or there may be a pun involved:

> Milkman: Are you sure you want twelve gallons of milk?
> Buyer: Yes, my doctor said that I have to take a bath in milk.
> Milkman: Do you want it pasteurized?
> Buyer: No, only up to my nose.

Or the question may set up an expectation from which the answer digresses, and the joke is on the listener: "Why do birds fly south for the winter? Because it's too far to walk." This kind of riddle is interesting to analyze because it requires thinking about subtleties of meaning and variations in sentence interpretation. This is an excellent exercise in semantics.

There are many ways for children to attend specifically to the form of language, and thereby increase their sensitivity to language structure. One sixth grader who had gone through a variety of these so-called consciousness-raising activities over a period of several months was asked to compare this work with his language arts textbook. He answered that in his book he learned *new* things, like nouns and verbs. "Where do you feel you learned more?" "Here," he replied. "Why?" "Because all this stuff makes you *think!*"

It is this kind of thinking, rather than mere facts of grammar, that contributes to linguistic awareness, and ultimately to language facility.

References

Chomsky, C. "Stages in Language Development and Reading Exposure." *Harvard Educational Review* 42 (February 1972): 1–33.

McCracken, R., and McCracken, M. *Reading Is Only the Tiger's Tail.* San Rafael, Calif.: Leswing Press, 1972.

Shipley, J. *Word Play.* New York: Hawthorn Books, 1972.

Grammar in the Language Arts Program

Carol Fisher
University of Georgia

Children must learn to use language effectively before learning to label words or sentences.

Constructing sentences with a variety of language structures should be the focus of grammatical instruction for children.

Formal usage patterns have a place in children's range of choices.

To have an effective language arts program, we should decide first what children must know and should be able to do at a given stage of development. These decisions then become the focus for learning and teaching. I believe we want children who can describe a special day so well that you almost feel you had been there. We want children who can look at a leaf and say or write, "It's dark green with a fuzzy surface and has points on the edges." Underlining *green* in a sentence with "green book" and labeling it *adj.* for *adjective* is not important. Our goal is the ability to describe things, not to identify descriptive words. We want children like fifth grader Benjamin Newland who can write:

> The Sunrise
>
> It slowly rises,
> As if reluctant to come up
> Its first rays touch the Earth,
> Then suddenly,
> Everywhere is light.

Does it matter whether he can tell that a sentence is compound or complex, declarative or interrogative or exclamatory? His description, touching our memories of a special sunrise, seems much more valuable than knowing that *slowly* and *suddenly* are adverbs or that *touch* is a transitive verb.

What is Grammar?

The term *grammar* means different things to different people. It is popularly used for the traditional Latinate practice of identifying parts of speech and choosing whether to say "doesn't" or "don't," "was" or "were." More recently in linguistic study, the word *grammar* has been used for the various systems that describe how our language operates, and the term *usage* refers to the different word choices we select to use. If we make this distinction, our concerns about children's "grammar" are centered mostly on helping them adopt the more socially correct usage choices. Labeling sentences or words, whether by parts of speech or form, and working with rules for transforming or generating sentences does not help children meet our primary objective of being able to form interesting and varied sentences in speech or writing.

Developing Sentence Construction Ability

There are several ways of helping children develop skill in using a variety of language structures in both speech and writing. Any of the activities recommended in this publication to develop children's language will directly or indirectly help them to form more varied and more complex kinds of language. There are also some particular activities that work precisely on these abilities in sentence construction, such as sentence expansion and sentence combination.

Expanding Sentences. The essential part of all activities involving sentence expansion is to help children learn how to add new information to their simple sentences. Instead of saying, "We went to the store," something could be added to tell which store: "We went to the new grocery store," or how the trip was made: "We went to the store in my brother's van," or who else went along: "We went to the store with my two cousins." All of these facts could even be put together into: "We went to the new grocery store in my brother's van with my two cousins."

Sentence expansion activities may be done as an experience story, with a small group of children giving ideas and suggesting ways of elaborating on the original sentence, while the teacher writes or prints the story for them—or the children may write their own additions. Sentence elaboration may also be done in a game format; for example, a child adds to the sentence before moving on a board game, or before making an *X* or *O* in a tic-tac-toe game. Teams may compete to see which can come up with an additional, further elaboration of the original, alternating until one team fails to think of something else to add.

Sentence Combining. The second major way of helping children become more skilled in constructing various kinds of sentences is through sentence combining activities. Here children learn many ways of putting together short, simple sentences. The sentence usually involves preplanned practice in which sentences of the same kind are combined by using the same device or structure. These exercises may be commercially produced or developed by the teacher. For example:

> Combine each of the pairs of sentences into one sentence using *with*.
>
> 1. The boy is late.   Answer: The boy with red hair
>   The boy has red hair.   is late.
> 2. The dog is mine.   Answer: The dog with a bone
>   The dog has a bone.   is mine.

Sentence combining activities can also be conducted in experience-story style, starting with the children's simple sentences describing something they've done, made, or observed. Typically this sentence combining activity is much less structured than planned practice exercises and it uses a variety of structures instead of focusing on one kind of combination.

Both sentence expanding and sentence combining should relate to children's own writing so that they can actively use what they learn. Group writing or composing is a particularly good way of helping children learn the process of putting ideas into writing. Here the teacher can list the children's ideas, discuss and plan how to combine and order them, talk about various ways of wording the ideas, and then write them down. Thus the process of writing is revealed.

Changing Language Usage Patterns

We are defining usage as the choices people make among the various ways of expressing their ideas. The selection depends on the situation, the audience, and on whether the language is written or oral. You might write a *no* as "I will be unable to attend because of previous commitments," but you might say this as, "I'm sorry I can't come. I've made other plans." When describing your classroom menace to the student's mother, you might say, "Lee still has some difficulty with self-control." To your principal, you might say, "Lee is still causing real problems with the other children," and to your best friend, "Lee's driving me crazy. No matter what I do, he's still hitting and pushing the other kids."

There really is no right or wrong usage. Usage choices are either appropriate for the situation or not appropriate; the choices are more or less formal, or more or less literate. Since children's language reflects the language they hear about them, telling children that "he don't" is wrong may present a conflict if that is what they hear at home. Besides, it isn't really wrong, just inappropriate for school. Thus, it is recommended that we help children accept the language they hear at home and in their neighborhood and at the same time add to their range of choices. Teachers may do this by first selecting the usage items that seem to be the most glaring—those that are the least socially acceptable. Then instead of saying, "Don't say 'he don't.' It's not right," say, "In school talk (or television talk) that would be 'he doesn't'." Ask the children to play roles in various situations and have them change their language—their usage—to fit the persons they're playing. Remind them that formal talks are a time for formal language. Read various materials to them so that they get a feel for how ideas are expressed in writing. In a group, write down what the children say, and then ask them to make the changes that would be made if the sayings were expressed in writing. Help children learn to adapt their language to the situation and to accept the language of their homes and families.

These recommendations are based on the primary goal of helping children become more and more adept at using language. The focus of the entire language arts program should be on having the children become truly skilled in expressing themselves, not on making them good at talking about language.

Part Two: Developing Writing Abilities

Part Two of this section presents three articles that focus on the development of writing ability. Learning about written language is seen as related but not identical to learning about spoken language. In the first article Bougere points out that learning to write begins with early scribblings, and early writing behavior closely parallels learning to speak. She describes classroom practices that can build on this early exploration and support further development. The next two articles present two different perspectives on fostering children's writing ability in school settings. Groff contends that while oral language development is important, growth in the ability to communicate does not end there. Differences between oral and written language dictate a special focus on the development of writing ability. Groff believes children can gain fluency in written language by helping them master the mechanics. A slightly different position is taken by Kantor. Allowing that the development of oral language does not ensure skill in writing, he emphasizes its importance as an entry to writing and advocates surrounding children's writing activities with much meaningful talk.

Growing into Writing

Marguerite Bougere
Tulane University

Writing begins with children's scribbles and develops through recognizable stages as children observe others who are writing, practice it themselves, and obtain helpful feedback.

Early writing experiences relate to learning to read as children come to understand how letters represent sounds and are combined to form words and whole utterances in a left-to-right sequence.

Twenty-eight-month-old Avron waved a scribbled sheet at his mother and said, "That says 'Stop!'"

Dougie, a five year old, presented his teacher with a drawing randomly surrounded by letters and letterlike forms, saying: "Give it to your children and learn them it, because it says a lot of fings" (Clay, p. 38).

Four-year-old Anne showed her nursery school teacher a drawing, under which were written two wavy lines of letters and letterlike scribbles. Saying she had written a story, she pointed to the left side of the first line of print and "read": "Peter peeked into the house. A bad ghost was inside. Peter scared the ghost away. The end." As she said "The end" Anne triumphantly jabbed the right-hand corner of the second line of print.

Avron, Dougie, and Anne had achieved the basic concept that writing conveys messages. Avron tried to reproduce a sign he and his mother had just seen in the street. Dougie was confident that his attempt at writing was valuable. Anne improvised a story and followed conventional left-to-right order in "reading" a message that no one else could decipher.

All the children had a long way to go before they could produce messages that were readable by others, but they were on the road to literacy. Their spontaneous scribbling was an important first step. And these children were fortunate indeed that the adults involved treated their approximations to writing with respect and encouragement.

The Beginning Stages of Writing

Research in early childhood learning shows that children can learn to write very much as they learn to speak: through observation, practice, and informal corrective feedback. Babies begin to take an interest in scribbling during the second year of life. When given a supportive environment for writing, and opportunities to scribble freely, children normally progress through observable stages of competency. Gibson and Levin cite that the quality of scribbling improves with practice, gradually becoming linear rather than randomly placed on the paper or slate, "and including more and more of the distinctive features of letters. . . ." When young children have letters and numbers available for copying spontaneously, they "make attempts to copy them and improve with time without correction or adult guidance. The child recognizes the better match himself and gets satisfaction from his improvement" (Gibson and Levin, p. 551).

When a child comes to us with an early scribble, we often fail to give it the acceptance that would encourage the child to grow naturally and confidently toward greater competence. Although parents and other adults talk to children and encourage them to respond long before they produce standard sentence forms, all too often, parents and preschool teachers either actively discourage scribbling or neglect to provide models and opportunities for practice. They fail to see learning to write as a developmental activity and are overly concerned with correctness.

Helping Preschoolers Grow into Writing

Writing materials such as pencils, crayons, felt-tipped pens, paper, slates, chalk, should be readily available where young children can get them on their own and use them. Books, alphabet sets, and the like should be available as models, and adults should become examples by writing themselves and occasionally joining in the child's writing games. They should encourage the child to dictate notes to family and friends, and treat the child's scribbles and approximations to writing with the same respect given to early attempts at verbal communication. Pressure for adult standards of accuracy should not be applied, any more than it should be when a child is beginning to talk, but support and active interest should be given.

In a developmental program the school provides the same kind of environment that helps writing growth in preschool years at home. Drawing, painting, and scribbling are encouraged and respected. As children develop, the teacher daily gives guidance and help to individuals in writing captions, sentences, and brief stories. The teacher can begin writing instructions by teaching children to write their own names in manuscript, and by giving group lessons on letter formation, along with individual work in helping children produce messages that are meaningful to them. Each child is given a notebook to write in daily. At first, actual writing is done by the teacher, at the child's dictation. For example, the child may draw something, and the teacher may write the caption. Then the teacher begins to ask the child to trace over the caption or other dictated material. As children grow in confidence and desire to write on their own, the teacher prepares material for copying. She writes down short dictations in well-spaced manuscript. She allows plenty of room for the child's early attempts to copy on lines below her model. No child is required to write to the point of fatigue or frustration. Perhaps a child may trace or copy only a word or two each day, while building toward proficiency and stamina in writing activites.

Along with growing ease in copying comes the ability to begin writing independently, and the teacher encourages independence by beginning sentences or stories for the child to finish alone. As fuller independence develops, the child may be given a personal "writing and spelling dictionary"—that is, a small notebook with each page headed by an alphabet letter—where the teacher can write new or special words the child asks for while writing. Each child's story is read and commented upon by the teacher, and individuals are encouraged to read their stories aloud or have the teacher read them during a group sharing period. Invented spellings are accepted by the teacher, who can use the written work to diagnose the child's progress in phonics and word identification skills. Such ongoing diagnosis can help the teacher plan useful skill work for group lessons in reading as well as in spelling and hand-writing. As individuals become fluent writers, the teacher can help them work toward greater mastery of correct form by having them correct and make clean copies of some of their writing for display or other special purposes.

Early Writing Aids Reading

The school beginner is in a stage of intellectual development that demands active involvement in learning activities. The production of messages in writing actively aids learning to read, as Marie Clay (1972, pp. 61–62) points out:

> The attention of eye and brain is directed to the elements of letters, to letter sequences and to spatial concepts. The child who writes a simple story is caught up in a process of synthesizing words and sentences. This building-up process is an excellent complement to the visual analysis of the text in . . . reading . . . which is a breaking-down process. By these two processes the child comes to understand the hierarchical relationships of letters, words, and utterances. He also confirms that the left-to-right constraint is applied to lines of print, to words within lines, and to letters within words.

Some years ago a thoughtful student of mine called writing "a neglected aspect of child development." Today, solid support for encouraging early writing comes from the studies of scholars such as Eleanor Gibson, Marie Clay, and Carol Chomsky, and from the success of early-education projects such as the High/Scope Educational Research Foundation. We have evidence that supportive environments can be provided to foster children's growth in writing as part of their total intellectual, social, and physical development.

References

Chomsky, Carol. "Write Now, Read Later," *Childhood Education* 47 (1971): 296–299.

Clay, Marie. *Reading: The Patterning of Complex Behaviour.* Auckland, New Zealand: Heinemann Educational Books, 1972.

Cognitively Oriented Curriculum: Writing and Reading. Ypsilanti, Mich.: High/Scope Educational Research Foundation, 1977.

Gibson, Eleanor J., and Levin, Harry. *The Psychology of Reading.* Cambridge, Mass.: M.I.T. Press, 1975.

Improving Children's Writing

Patrick Groff
San Diego State University

Skill in written composition is not the inevitable and natural result of oral language development; it requires specific practice and instruction.

To develop good writers, teachers must provide motivation for writing, instruction in handwriting and spelling skills, constructive responses to compositions, and an audience for what children write.

There appears to be no indirect route to the full development of written composition skills. Skill in writing will not simply emerge as a result of the natural development of oral language. Therefore, teachers should not depend completely on their instruction in oral language. They need to consider some appropriate, more direct means for developing writing.

Written composition skills must be taught, as such, because children's writing is a separate linguistic matter from their oral language. These two means of expression differ in both structure and manner of functioning. For example, writing does not repeat the developmental stages of speech, and learning to write is different from learning to talk.

Furthermore, we know that written language is not simply a recording of oral language. Other research raises even deeper doubts as to the very close and highly positive relationships between oral and written language that some experts say exist. These points remind us of the need to identify, as specifically as possible, what teachers can do to influence children's writing. Of the many teaching activities that have been offered, four appear to have the greatest validity.

The foremost recommendation is that children must be motivated if they are to write effectively. This comment is confirmed by all that is known of the psychology of learning. The trouble is that, in many schools, the circumstances do not encourage composition, and children's urges to write are somewhat short-lived. Each time they undertake a new writing task, the teacher must find fresh ways of stimulating their interests. While this is a responsibility of no small order, it is often passed over or slighted because of the demands of time and the limits of the teacher's ingenuity. Fortunately, there are now many books that give suggestions for stimulating children's writing. (Some of these are included at the end of this article.) In these texts, teachers can find ways of exciting children about an almost limitless variety of writing assignments.

Opportunities for writing experiences are numerous in classrooms that have access to television, film, magazines, pictures, manipulative materials, collections, and specimens of various kinds. The classroom that gives the impression of a workshop or laboratory is also a great stimulus for things to write about. Then, the teacher who uses children's expressed interests as a basis for their writing will find that they write more and more.

The second obligation of the teacher is to help children with the physical act of putting words down on paper. Recent research shows that children's control of the mechanics of writing relates to the quality of what they write. One such study, from the National Assessment of Educational Progress, found that children who do well with the basic mechanics of writing are also those who write with the most ingenuity. While no cause and effect relationship may be assumed, it may very well be that confidence in the mechanics of writing releases children to produce original, creative compositions.

What is true for handwriting can be extended to spelling. Many children are unenthusiastic about composition unless they are confident that they can spell most of the words they want to write. The teacher thus needs to conduct effective programs in both handwriting and spelling.

There are several ways of helping reduce the difficulty of writing. Younger children may enjoy dictating their stories or other kinds of writing to older children, parent volunteers, aides, or the teacher. Knowledge of phonics helps the child write words. The teacher who circulates among the students during the writing period to jot down spellings for children is wiser than the one who directs them to the dictionary for this purpose. Teachers can also make children's writing easier by not being overly critical about matters such as paragraphing, evenness of margins, the niceties of punctuation, or proper word-division at the ends of lines. Teachers can accept children's use of their own dialectical patterns and usage without correcting them. Children find that writing on every other line allows an open space for making corrections or revisions.

A third important responsibility of the teacher in the development of children's writing is to respond critically and constructively to what they write. Putting grades on children's papers does not help them learn how to improve their writing. Instead, children need specific suggestions as to how some aspects of their writing can be improved, and about things they have done well.

Such critical suggestions are best made in an individual conference with the child-author. While it is inappropriate to contrast children's writing with mature models, it is proper to use previous writings of pupils as one confers with them. Accordingly, the teacher can use checklists to ask of each successive writing by the child: Has the content improved? Is it better organized? Is there a greater variety of vocabulary? Are the sentences more varied and grammatical? Is it a more honest expression of the child's personality, status, and experiences? Does it exhibit a greater degree of personal enthusiasm, satisfaction, or gratification? Is it more sensitive to the needs of the argument, the narrative, or the audience for whom it is intended? Children should be encouraged to ask the same questions about their own papers, and to "proof" them by reading aloud what they have written.

On the basis of the kinds of critical questions asked of children about their writings, the teacher can propose increasingly more changes in their writings as time passes. Negative criticism offered in this manner does not discourage children. Sometimes these changes can be made by children directly onto the first copy by using the "spare line" tactic described earlier. At other times, children may see the need for a cleaner copy and will rewrite their paper. This is especially suitable when their compositions are collected and put into books, prepared for display, or taken home. Teachers need to be sensitive as to how the child feels about any particular piece of writing. How well that child understands the teacher's suggestions for revision is of the greatest importance.

A final consideration for teachers in developing children's writing skill is the need to find some kind of audience for the writing. Children need recognition from classmates, from other children in their school, and from parents and other adults. This sharing can take the form of classroom or school displays of their written work. Their compositions can be copied into "books" for other classes or parents to read. A class can produce a literary magazine or an occasional booklet of their writings. Also, children's written products, like those of adult writers, can be read, talked about, and analyzed for literary merit. In these ways, children receive feedback about their work as writers. They learn what succeeds and what needs improvement. Having others read what children write gives them added purpose and motivation for more writing.

References

Bennett, Neville. *Teaching Styles and Pupil Progress.* Cambridge, Mass.: Harvard University Press, 1976.

Groff, Patrick. "Does Negative Criticism Discourage Children's Compositions?" *Language Arts, 52* (October 1975):1032-34.

Groff, Patrick. "Children's Oral Language and Their Written Composition." *Elementary School Journal, 78* (January 1978):180-91.

Additional Resources

Attea, Mary. *Turning Children on through Creative Writing.* Buffalo, N.Y.: DOK, 1973.

Barbe, William. *Creative Writing Activities.* Columbus, Ohio: Highlights, 1965.

Carlson, Ruth. *Sparkling Words: Two Hundred Twenty-Five Practical and Creative Writing Ideas.* Champaign, Ill.: National Council of Teachers of English, 1973.

Carlson, Ruth. *Writing Aids through the Grades: One Hundred Eighty-Six Developmental Writing Activities.* New York: Teachers College, Columbia University, 1970.

Esbensen, Barbara. *Celebration of Bees.* Minneapolis: Winston, 1975.

Gerbrandt, Gary. *Idea Book for Acting Out and Writing Language K-8.* Champaign, Ill.: National Council of Teachers of English, 1974.

Hennings, Dorothy. *Content and Craft: Written Expression in the Elementary School.* Englewood Cliffs, N. J.: Prentice-Hall, 1973.

Hughes, Ted. *Poetry in the Making.* Salem, N. H.: Faber and Faber, 1967.

Koch, Kenneth. *Wishes, Lies and Dreams: A New Way of Teaching Children to Write Poetry.* New York: Random House, 1970.

McAllister, Constance. *Creative Writing for Beginners.* Columbus, Ohio: Highlights, 1976.

Moore, Walter. *A Thousand Topics for Composition.* Champaign, Ill.: National Council of Teachers of English, 1971.

Petty, Walter, and Bowen, Mary. *Slithery Snakes and Other Aids to Children's Writing.* Englewood Cliffs, N. J.: Prentice-Hall, 1969.

Slaudacker, Carol. *Creative Writing in the Classroom.* San Francisco: Fearon, 1968.

Tiedt, Iris. *Individualizing Writing in the Elementary Classroom.* Champaign, Ill.: National Council of Teachers of English, 1975.

Talking as an Entry into Writing

Kenneth J. Kantor
University of Georgia

Developing children's oral language will not ensure skill in writing, but it may enhance the growth of writing ability.

Instruction in writing at beginning levels should aim at extending the fluency, personal voice, and sense of audience already initiated in oral language expression.

Recently a number of language researchers have been looking at relationships between talking and writing and have noted some important differences between the two. In speech, for example, we usually receive immediate response to what we're saying, whereas in writing we often must imagine our audience and try to anticipate their reactions. Also, the written word usually involves more of a commitment, so we tend to be more concerned with "getting it right" than when we are speaking. These differences and others have led some educators to conclude that teaching writing requires methods that are quite distinct from those used in teaching oral language.

We ought not assume, however, that children's speaking abilities are of little value in helping them learn to write. While we cannot depend solely on oral language instruction for teaching writing as well, we should take advantage of the many opportunities which talk provides for entries into writing experiences. In other words, the child's skill in speaking is a key that can unlock the front door of the writing house, even though it may not unlock all doors within the house. As Nancy Martin (1976) and her associates reveal, talk enables us to communicate basic needs, establish and maintain relationships with others, develop our own identities, understand how and why things happen as they do, predict what will happen in new situations, and simply have fun. All of these traits are true of writing as well; and to the extent that they have been developed through oral language, they will enhance the growth of writing ability.

In fact, some of the key terms we use to describe effective writing have their basis in oral expression. One of these is *fluency*, or the ability to write smoothly and at times even effortlessly. This fluency or language flow develops mostly as a result of numerous and varied opportunites for talk, especially informal conversation and discussion. A second important factor is *personal voice*, or the extent to which the writer "speaks" to his or her audience as one human being who has something to say to another. Personal voice is revealed by traits such as honesty, clarity, and simplicity; writers seek to share something with their readers rather than trying to impress them with any particular knowledge or skill. Again, children find their own voices primarily through good experiences in speaking. Finally, we often refer to good writers as having a *sense of audience*. They form an image of what their readers will understand and enjoy, and thus make sound judgments as to the content, organization, and style that will appeal to those readers. And what better chance for children to develop this audience awareness than in talking with each other and with trusted adults?

Specifically, talking serves as an important prewriting activity, as a procedure for helping children generate ideas before they write. This brainstorming process can help children warm up to the writing task, as they develop the raw material for their writing. One teacher (and writer) who uses this method effectively is Barbara Esbensen (1975) as she asks a series of questions to draw out children's images and ideas on a subject (the city, the seasons, animals) and then records children's responses in clusters on the chalkboard to guide them toward producing vivid and imaginative poetry. The many excellent examples of children's poems cited in her book *A Celebration of Bees* illustrate the success of her prewriting method—the value of talking before writing. At the same time we ought to recognize the warning of Phillip Lopate (1978), another teacher and poet, that we should avoid so-called overkill in prewriting discussion. Sometimes such a discussion generates so much excitement that the writing seems anticlimactic to children; the writing task may then seem more like drudgery than a pleasurable activity. Teachers need to make careful judgments as to how much talk is enough to provide motivation and ideas for writing, but not so much as to diminish their students' interest.

Given the usefulness of talk as an entry into writing, we still face the question of whether children can write effectively if they haven't mastered the mechanical skills of handwriting, spelling, and punctuation. My opinion is that while these skills are certainly helpful for beginning writing, they are not crucial. Children can write with some degree of fluency, if not mechanical accuracy, as early as the preschool years. Many children may feel self-conscious about mechanics, especially spelling, because parents or teachers place undue emphasis on those narrower skills. Worrying about spelling or punctuation may even interrupt the flow of their language, and children can thereby lose a good image or idea or phrasing. If we can cause children simply to produce as much written language as possible without their being preoccupied with mechanics, we can help them develop the fluency necessary to feel comfortable and confident with writing.

Fluency requires our giving children many opportunities for writing practice, especially of the so-called free-writing kind in which they record thoughts as quickly as they come into their minds, and establish a rhythm and flow of writing. The purpose of frequent writing practice is to make writing seem almost as natural as talking. Once some ease and confidence are established, we can help children with those mechanical aspects of writing that shape and refine the product and make it more effective. It's not that mechanics are unimportant, but that fluency must come first. In turn, fluent writing provides a real reason to learn to spell, capitalize, and punctuate.

Direct personal experiences provide the best source of material for children's writing and they enable them to speak and write in their own voices. We should encourage children to write about baseball or little sisters or favorite songs or places or about going fishing or making new friends or anything else they have something to say about. And in respecting the values of these experiences, we should respond positively to children's expressions of thought and feeling that touch chords in our own experience.

Finally, we should help children develop a sense of audience through sharing their writing with others, especially with each other. Writing only to a teacher audience leads to undue concern with producing what the teacher wants, and too little with expressing one's own thoughts honestly and directly. A more important role for the teacher is that of guiding small groups of students in sharing their writing and responding to each other. In this way, children begin to acquire an awareness of the effects their writing may have on various audiences.

Elements of good writing thus have important parallels in oral language that can be extended and applied to writing. As we encourage children to express ideas with fluency, personal voice, and sense of audience, so will we foster their growth in writing ability.

References

Martin, Nancy, et al. "From Talk to Writing." In *Writing and Learning Across the Curriculum*. London: Ward Lock Educational, 1976.

Esbensen, Barbara. *A Celebration of Bees: Helping Children to Write Poetry*. Minneapolis: Winston Press, 1975.

Lopate, Phillip. "Helping Young Children Start to Write." In *Research on Composing*, edited by C. Cooper and L. Odell, pp. 135-149. Urbana, Ill.: National Council of Teachers of English, 1978.

Additional Resources

Burrows, Alvina; Jackson, Doris; and Saunders, Dorothy. *They All Want to Write*. New York: Holt, Rinehart, 1964.

Carlson, Ruth. *Sparkling Words: 225 Practical and Creative Writing Ideas*. Geneva, Ill.: Paladin House, 1973.

Clay, Marie. *What Did I Write?* London: Heinemann Books, 1972.

Clegg, A. B., ed. *The Excitement of Writing*. London: Chatto and Windus, 1969.

Dodd, Anne Wescott. *Write Now! Insights Into Creative Writing*. New York: Globe Book Company, 1973.

Evertts, Eldonna, ed. *Explorations in Children's Writing*. Urbana, Ill.: National Council of Teachers of English, 1970.

Holbrook, David. *Children's Writing*. Cambridge, Mass.: Harvard University Press, 1967.

Koch, Kenneth. *Wishes, Lies and Dreams: Teaching Children to Write Poetry*. New York: Vintage Books, 1970.

Kohl, Herbert. *Teaching the "Unteachable": The Story of an Experiment in Children's Writing*. New York: The New York Review, 1967.

Lopate, Phillip. *Being with Children*. New York: Doubleday, 1975.

Moffett, James. *A Student-Centered Language Arts Curriculum, Grades K-6*. Boston: Houghton Mifflin, 1968.

Petty, Walter, and Bowen, Mary. *Slithery Snakes and Other Aids to Children's Writing*. New York: Appleton-Century-Crofts, 1967.

Synectics, Inc. *Making It Strange*. Books 1-4. New York: Harper and Row, 1968.

Part Three: Developing Reading Abilities

Learning about language is part of learning about the world. As children have experiences with written language—listening to stories, watching others write, noticing signs and symbols in the environment, and experimenting with reading—they develop concepts that have significance for developing reading abilities. Part Three presents a series of articles that explore various aspects of how children learn to read. Goodman examines the beginnings of reading and presents the results of research in young children's awareness of print in the environment. Pinnell's article describes how children become sensitive to the patterns and characteristics of written language as they have experiences with books. Smith explores the relationship between children's knowledge of the structure of language and their facility in reading comprehension. He focuses on the reader's knowledge of vocabulary and syntactic structures. Taking a different view, Terry cautions against teaching skills in isolation, and advocates giving children many opportunities to read books as the primary concern of the reading teacher.

Reading—How Does It Begin?

Yetta Goodman
University of Arizona

Bess Altwerger
University of New Mexico

Preschoolers already know a great deal about print and many are able to "read" the words they encounter in familiar situations.

Isolating the components of written language by presenting letters, words, and phrases out of a real context makes reading an abstract and difficult task.

An environment that is rich in experiences with books, magazines, and other printed matter, and the writing of stories and personal letters provide the encounters with written language from which children learn to read.

On any day of the week in New York City, Detroit, Chicago, Tucson, or Los Angeles, it is easy to find a five-year-old reaching across the deli counter to pay for the items on the grocery list, or a nine-year-old explaining to her three-year-old brother that they must wait until that sign says walk before they may cross the street, or a preschool-age consumer sneaking a box of Count Chocula cereal into the shopping cart while Mom isn't looking. Behind apartment doors, one can find a five-year-old choosing a can of tuna for lunch while Mom's at work, or a toddler watching the words fly across the television screen during commercials for hours on end, or a little boy who is cuddling up to Grandma for a bedtime story.

What all these familiar scenes have in common is that the children are involved with and using written language within meaningful and functional settings. They know that print communicates— that it "says" something, that it's supposed to make sense, and even that it's sequenced from left to right. Children have learned this because in our society they and all of us are surrounded by print. It has become a necessary part of our communication system, and children as well as adults interact with it almost every day of their lives. Nobody has to teach preschoolers what they learn about print before entering kindergarten, just as nobody has to teach them how to speak and understand oral language. Children are masters at making sense of their world, and today written language is a vital part of that world for most children in the United States.

Over the years, articles and books on beginning reading have suggested that some children learn to read before entering school. Delores Durkin (1966) reported an important retrospective study of children who read before beginning school, but in most cases, children such as these are regarded as unusual. It is generally assumed that most children, especially those living in urban inner-city environments or from lower socioeconomic backgrounds, cannot read or meaningfully interact with print before they are taught in school.

Since 1973, both formal and informal studies have been conducted in Arizona, Michigan, Indiana, and Ontario to determine preschoolers' awareness of print in their environment and in books, their concepts of reading and writing, and their writing ability (Goodman and Cox, 1978; Goodman and Goodman, 1979). The children in these studies were two to five years old and represented a variety of ethnic, linguistic, and socioeconomic backgrounds. Awareness of environmental print was determined by asking the children to respond to print such as that on food and household product labels, street signs, and store signs. In some cases the actual sign or box was used. Later the print became less and less contextualized, as the first task consisted of print accompanied by pictures and symbols, the second included only the stylized logo, and the third consisted only of the words in black-and-white manuscript form. The children were asked "What does this say?" and "Show me where it says that."

The purpose of this paper is not to present detailed statistical analyses from the research, but rather to discuss general findings concerning what children know about written language by the time they come to school and to suggest what this means for classroom instruction.

The most important finding is that preschoolers are able to react meaningfully to print in their environment. Most very young children can tell what a stop sign says even when they see only a picture of one. Children develop an awareness that print has directionality. When a child is looking at a cereal box and responds appropriately with "That says Cheerios," often the child will point to the print, moving a finger along the row of letters. Most children will respond in a functional way to the print they are familiar with. "I brush my teeth with that," a four year old might say while pointing to C-R-E-S-T, or "That says buy cars" in response to a picture of a large automobile while pointing to a small logo of a nationally known automobile in the upper left-hand corner.

Young children make a functional or appropriate response to print seen within a familiar context but when the context is unfamiliar, trying to decipher it is treated as a strange task. Children who are three, four, or five years old, for example, are good at responding to *Crest* when it is printed in the familiar blue letters on the toothpaste box, but when they are shown *Crest* printed in manuscript on a white card, the response indicates that what they see is unrelated letters or nonsense. The print on the card has no meaning for them. Some children respond by saying "I can't read" while others act bored and want to get away from the activity.

Another important finding is that preschool children seem to be more aware of the function of print on objects in their environment than they are of the function of print in books. Children who are very comfortable with responding appropriately to familiar print in their environment may not know, when being read to, that the print in books is what tells the story. Often when asked "Show me where I am reading" the child will respond by pointing to the illustrations on the picture page. When asked what the print is on the page, they may say "letters," "words," or "numbers" as if it had nothing to do with the reading. It seems, however, that children who have had much experience in being read to in an intimate, one-to-one setting are more aware of the function of print in books than those who have been read to in large group situations or not at all.

Children develop concepts and knowledge about the world through their interaction with the things that are part of their surroundings. Thus, when written language, books, magazines, personal letters, are part of their world, children develop concepts and knowledge about written language.

Based on these considerations, we must raise serious questions about the concept of so-called reading readiness as it is applied in most schools. Programs around the country are aimed at "getting a child ready" to read. Although the child has already begun to

organize concepts about what print is and how it is used by interacting with it in meaningful and functional settings, reading
readiness programs may present letters, words, and phrases out
of linguistic and situational contexts and tell children that this is
what reading is all about. Interaction with books, pencils, newspapers, personal letters, and the like, is often delayed until the
child does something that is assumed to be prerequisite to reading.

The children we have studied and worked with have received no
formal instruction, yet they have begun to read. Reading may be
its own readiness. Rich experiences with books, magazines, signs
and symbols in the environment, and with writing stories and
personal letters may be the environment in which not only readiness occurs but reading begins to develop. Children learn language
by interacting with it in meaningful contexts and through using it
to communicate in social settings. Language use—both oral and
written—can be its own teacher.

What can the classroom teacher do to encourage and extend
what children already know about written language upon entering
school? The teacher must not confuse them! Children expect
written language to make sense and to be a part of meaningful
situations. Setting up a literate classroom environment, in which
written language is a means of communication and not an end in
itself, will nurture the common-sense notions about print that
children bring to school.

Teachers should encourage children to use their knowledge of
print when drawing or constructing models of their neighborhoods, playing in the classroom play store or house, shopping,
reading labels, and following directions for a cooking project.
Children can write notes to send through the classroom mailbox,
write captions explaining their art work, or keep a diary or journal.
In some cases children might dictate their stories to the teacher,
but in general, the writing process should develop on its own.

Our research suggests that children need first-hand, individual or
small-group experiences with books. Books should be read to the
children to show them where the story is coming from. They
should leaf through books on their own, and become familiar with
how books work. And of course, one of the best ways for children
to learn about books is for them to become authors themselves.

Most importantly, written language must be presented to the
children as a whole, meaningful communication system. Fragment-
ing and isolating components of written language makes reading
an abstract and difficult task.

We need further research on children's developing awareness of print. This can be done in both informal and formal settings. Teachers in the classroom can observe children as they respond to print in their environment (Goodman, 1978). What do children think is written on certain offices or cabinets in the school? On a walk around the school yard, what do the signs along the curb or at the school entrance say? When children are looking through books, magazines, or newspapers, how do they show the degree of their awareness of the function and purpose of these materials?

It's time for teachers to learn from the children, watch what they do as they interact with print, encourage their inquiry, and respect and extend all of the experiences and knowledge about written language that children bring to the classroom.

References

Durkin, D. *Children Who Read Early.* New York: Teachers College Press, 1966.

Goodman, K. S., and Goodman, Y. M. "Learning to Read Is Natural." In *Theory and Practice of Early Reading*, Vol. 1, edited by L. B. Resnick and P. Weaver. Hillsdale, N.J.: Erlbaum Associates, 1979.

Goodman, Y. M. "Kid Watching: An Alternative to Testing." *The National Elementary Principal* (June 1978): 41–5.

Goodman, Y. M., and Cox, V. *A Study of the Development of Literacy in Preschool Children.* Tucson: University of Arizona Research Project Proposal, 1978.

Read, C. *Children's Categorization of Speech Sounds in English.* Urbana, Ill.: National Council of Teachers of English, 1975.

Developing the Awareness of Book Language

Gay Su Pinnell
Ohio State Department of Education

Learning to read involves learning that written language is different from spoken language.

As children have many experiences with different kinds of written language, they become more sensitive to the features of written language—the language of books.

Many children pretend to "read" stories that they have heard before. Sometimes, if the story is very familiar, they almost "read" it word for word. As they read in this way, they reveal their understanding of some ways in which the language of stories is different from the language of everyday talk. And learning about book language is an important part of learning to read, independently, material that is unfamiliar.

As children hear stories read aloud they sometimes repeat words or phrases as they respond to particular patterns of language. During a reading of "The Three Bears" you will often hear children saying the "Who's been sleeping in my bed?" part. Or young children may repeat phrases such as "good night, house; good night, mouse" after a few readings of *Goodnight Moon* by Margaret Wise Brown. They can describe details in pictures or a sequence of events, such as those in *Rosie's Walk* by Hutchins. We often hear children chiming in on the "once upon a time" or "and they all lived happily ever after" parts of a story. Three-year-old Jenny was fascinated by the "Plop!" when a pile of snow was dumped on Peter's head in *The Snowy Day*. She requested the story often, and when her mother came to that page, she would slap her head with her hand, shouting "Plop!"

As children have more experience with books and stories they begin to develop notions of what a "story" is, and of structure, and patterns not normally used in their spoken language. They become more sensitive to repetition and to sounds of words. Parents and preschool teachers often notice young children "reading" a book by looking at the pictures, carefully turning the pages, and inventing their own stories to express the meaning they find.

The invented stories are likely to describe actions or details in pictures; and if they've heard the story frequently, the children may repeat specific words or phrases from the actual text of the story.

Observing and Listening to Children

Five-year-old Jenny (the "Plop" fan) has had a rich background of experience with books. Observing her behavior and listening to her retelling of a story can reveal much about her growing awareness of book language.

She loves the story *Where the Wild Things Are* by Maurice Sendak. She has heard it many times. After one such re-reading her mother asked Jenny to "read" the story. Jenny's invented version began with "Once upon a time," indicating that she had heard many stories and was comfortable using a standard device for starting them. Jenny went on to describe details in the pictures, using her own everyday language:

Text: The night Max wore his wolf suit and made mischief of one kind and another his mother called him "WILD THING" and Max said, "I'LL EAT YOU UP!" so he was sent to bed without eating anything.

Jenny: Once upon a time there was a little boy named Max. He was hanging on a rope, tied. His room was a mess. Max made a picture. It was a picture of a monster. It says by Max, and there was steps and there was a dog.

As Jenny moved further into the story she began to display an increased sense of drama and audience. In several instances she used the actual language of the text:

Text: . . . sailed off through night and day and in and out of weeks and almost over a year to where the wild things are.

Jenny: And then Max said, "Well, I think I'll take my boat." The wild things said [hesitation] and in, out of weeks and over, over a year to where the wild things are. And then Max said to the wild things, "I hate you!"

Frequently Jenny displayed awareness of the patterns of language in the story and used them in new ways:

Text: . . . roared their terrible roars and gnashed their terrible teeth and rolled their terrible eyes and showed their terrible claws til Max said, "BE STILL."

Jenny: They roared their terrible roars. *They stomped their terrible feet.* They blinked their eyes at them eighty times . . . and then he said, "Well, I think *I'll crunch my terrible teeth!* I'm gonna eat you up!"

At one point in the story Jenny seemed to produce a sequence that sounded like the text rather than one that had meaning for her:

Text: . . . over a year and in and out of weeks and through a day and into the night of his own room where he found his supper waiting for him and it was still hot.

Jenny: . . . and sailed back over a year without of weeks and throughout the day. Into the night of his very own room where he found his supper waiting for him and he was happy and it was still hot.

Jenny ended her story exactly as did the author. The last phrase, ". . . and it was still hot," is one that had special meaning for her and is frequently repeated verbatim by children.

Jenny was also recorded while retelling a story she had just heard for the first time. Her mother read *In the Rabbitgarden* by Leo Lionni and then asked Jenny to tell the story as she looked through the book. As before, Jenny began by describing details in the pictures:

Jenny: There were two rabbits together and one big one. One had black eyes with a brown circle. One had brown eyes with a brown circle. And one had brown eyes with a pink circle. Then the orange one with the black circle and the black one with the black circle went off to look for carrots.

Compared with the previous story, however, fewer segments of the retelling were similar to the text.

Careful examination of Jenny's story retelling can reveal much about her awareness of the features of written language. She can "talk like a book," an ability that Marie Clay (1972) describes as an important step in learning to read. She has notions of sequence, story construction, and the patterns and structures of written language. Above all, she is interacting with written language in a way that is meaningful to her. Jenny expects to be able to read independently soon, and she expects to get meaning from what she reads. She is beginning to learn to read by making full use of her knowledge of language.

Learning about Book Language

Any discussion of reading or learning to read must be based on the notion that written language is first and foremost *language*. When children learn to read and write, they are learning about language; they are learning a particular use of language. Children who have many experiences with written language soon learn that "our use of the language when we speak differs from our use in written form" (Clay, 1972). All children, whatever dialect or variety of language they speak in their homes, must become aware of the differences between spoken language and book language. Like knowledge of spoken language, knowledge of book language is developed as children experience it, respond to it, and try to use it in their daily lives.

Children are surrounded by a world of written language. They see in their environments a variety of written language—signs, advertisements, newspapers, books, and so on—which they try to make sense of and to use. As young children have experiences with books, they become aware of the features of the written language they encounter. They bring to the reading situation everything they know about language and they learn new patterns and meanings as they gain experience.

Observing and listening to children as they respond to written language can help parents and teachers become sensitive to children's knowledge of book language. We can often learn more through informal interactions with children than we can through so-called readiness tests or formal diagnostic procedures. Some fruitful activities for gathering evidence of awareness of book language are:

> Read a story to a child and then ask the child to "read" or tell the story while looking at the pages.
>
> Record the language and listen to it again. Try doing this once a week for three or four weeks.
>
> Observe children as they dramatize a story that has been read to them.
>
> Examine children's dictated stories for evidence of book language.
>
> Read a story that children have previously heard. At some point ask them to try to predict what the next page will say. (Be careful not to overdo this and ruin the story.)

Extend stories through activities such as painting, clay, or collage and listen as children talk while they work.

Helping Children Grow in Language

It is important to remember that awareness of book language is developed through experiences with written language. Jenny had many opportunities to hear stories, and her favorite ones were read over and over to her. Not all children may have so much literary input. For all children, the school situation should offer many opportunities for experiences with written language. Reading stories aloud to children, among many other benefits, makes the patterns of written language available for their use and helps build knowledge of book language. Children should be encouraged to take books home for their parents, other adults, or older brothers and sisters to read to them.

Children need to hear a variety of written language. They need to hear stories and other written materials that use language similar to their spoken language; they also need exposure to written language that differs from their spoken language. They need stories that offer description and dialogue, and they need to hear the language of fairy tales and fantasy. Stories with repetition of words and phrases—not the stilted language of some basal readers, but that which occurs naturally as part of storytelling—are especially helpful to the youngster who is just becoming acquainted with book language.

Children need everyday experiences with all kinds of books. They learn best in a stimulating but informal atmosphere. Above all, they need the presence of a sensitive adult who can enjoy books with them and can make book language and the meanings inherent in written language readily available. Browsing through books, hearing stories read aloud, talking, telling stories (perhaps having them written down), and encountering new and interesting features of written language—all provide a curriculum for developing children's awareness of the language of books.

References

Clay, Marie. *Reading: The Patterning of Complex Behavior.* Auckland, New Zealand: Heinemann Educational Books, 1972.

Huck, Charlotte S. *Children's Literature in the Elementary School,* 3rd ed. New York: Holt, Rinehart and Winston, 1976.

McKenzie, Moira, and Warlow, Aidan, eds. *Reading Matters: Selecting and Using Books in the Classroom.* London: Hodder and Stoughton in Association with Inner London Education Authority, 1977.

Additional Resources

Brown, Margaret Wise. *Goodnight Moon.* New York: Harper and Row, 1947.

Hutchins, Pat. *Rosie's Walk.* New York: Macmillan, 1968.

Keats, Ezra Jack. *The Snowy Day.* New York: Viking, 1962.

Lionni, Leo. *In the Rabbitgarden.* New York: Pantheon, 1975.

Sendak, Maurice. *Where the Wild Things Are.* New York: Scholastic, 1963.

Language Awareness and Reading Comprehension

William Smith
University of Pittsburgh

Reading comprehension is related to the reader's knowledge of the vocabulary and syntactic structures used in the material.

Children can learn new words and structures through reading if the relationship between the two is carefully controlled.

Reading is too often viewed as just something to be taught or as a way of testing achievement. Indeed, we are responsible for teaching reading in schools and it is one way of assessment, but those are not the most important reasons for including reading in the curriculum. Reading is a means by which children and adults can learn new ideas. At the same time, reading is highly related to children's knowledge of the meaning and structure of language and it is a valuable tool for enriching language development.

Before children learn to read, they already have acquired most of the basic syntactic rules of the language and they have learned a considerable number of words. As they develop reading abilities, they must learn to combine language structures with ease and to use them in varied ways. How much they will comprehend depends partly on their working vocabulary and on the language structures and patterns they are able to use effectively.

The single most important variable in reading comprehension, as assessed by most commonly used measures, is the students' knowledge of the meanings of words in the material being read—their basic knowledge of vocabulary. As students mature, their knowledge of vocabulary increases in two ways. First, new words are learned through interaction with other speakers, from school in general, and from reading. The first meanings attached to these new words are usually limited to denotations and are only approximations of what adults know about the words. Indeed, applying these first, limited meanings may sometimes actually restrict the students' comprehension at the literal level.

After new words are learned, children must learn additional meanings and shades of meaning for each word. As children encounter a word more often, they are forced to learn its connotations as well as denotations; they learn how the word can be used in new contexts. These additional meanings are crucial to the students' ability to comprehend on the inference level.

The learning process is actually somewhat cyclical; the more words a reader knows, the more words that reader can infer from the context about words that are unknown. If a student is asked to read a passage in which there are a number of unknown words, comprehension is seriously impeded. If only one or two words are unknown, the meanings can at least partially be inferred from the context. It has long been observed that students can read at a level that seems to surpass their ability to write or speak. Actually, students may be unable to enunciate specifically all words on a page, but they may be able to handle reading material that is "rich in context"—that is, containing many words that have meaning for the student. When attempting to read materials that are rich in context, students are able to guess at the meanings of unknown words or even "read around" those words without seriously decreasing comprehension.

Knowledge of the structures and patterns of language is also related to understanding and using context to gain meaning from reading. Familiarity with the syntax of the language in the material being read is an important factor in whether the reader can use context effectively. We have ample evidence that as students mature, they are able to read and comprehend increasingly more complex sentences. It seems that readers in the early grades understand what they are reading more easily if the material contains language with structures consistent with their own talk. At the beginning levels, students seem to read each sentence as if it were the entire passage and they have some difficulty in processing large amounts of verbal material at once. Structures in the speech and writing of young children are not as complex as those of older children and adults. Sentences are often linked with *and* or *and then*, for example, "I went downtown, and I bought a toy car, and it was a Corvette, and then I took it home, and then I showed it to my friend Bobby."

Using reading material with simple language structures increases comprehension for beginning readers, but it also creates a problem which can decrease comprehension. As mentioned above, context is very important for determining the basic meaning of an unknown word and for elaborating the meaning of a known word. Because young readers sometimes tire and frustrate quickly, length of passages they are asked to read is often limited. Consequently, the simple sentences typically found in readers designed for beginners are lacking in the context necessary to guess at meaning.

The delicate issue, then, is: How complex should the sentence be? The issue is resolved by determining the purpose of reading. If we want students to read with high accuracy and easy comprehension, then simple (but natural) sentences are best, and materials should be generally consistent with the language which students speak or write. However, if we want children to learn new ideas from the reading, then sentences must be made more complex (by adding adjectives, adverbs, and clauses), to enlarge the context and provide sufficient information for the student to guess at unknown words.

Thus, a general pattern emerges. As students grow in their ability to read, their vocabulary increases as does their ability to comprehend more complex structures. When using reading as a means of learning new information or as a means of testing, it is extremely important that the teacher know the language development level of each child. While we know that young children read simple sentences best, we also know that more advanced students may actually have trouble reading sentences that are too simple. These students expect sentences to be complex and have learned how to interrelate the sentences. Therefore, if the syntax does not fit their expectations, they are forced to slow down. In effect, they must rewrite the sentences in their heads while they read. This slowing down not only creates boredom, it often causes a lack of attention; the untaxed mind wanders. Consequently, these students may not comprehend well and their learning is limited.

The implication of this research on the effect of language on reading comprehension is that we are dealing with a two-edged sword. The stage of the child's language development is related to how much of the material will be understood at both literal and inferential levels. Further, language development will affect the efficiency (speed as well as comprehension) of reading. The other edge of the sword is pedagogical. We know that both vocabulary and syntax can affect comprehension, and we know that introducing too much of the unknown into reading material will create insurmountable difficulties. By carefully controlling one factor, we can increase the difficulty of the other, thus allowing the student to gain in knowledge without creating frustration or boredom. As a consequence, reading becomes a systematic tool for acquiring and developing language, and this new linguistic ability allows us to continue the cycle.

References

Guthrie, John T., ed. *Cognition, Curriculum and Comprehension.* Newark, Del.: International Reading Association, 1977.

Johnson, Dale D., and Pearson, P. David. *Teaching Reading Vocabulary.* New York: Holt, Rinehart and Winston, 1978.

Pearson, P. David, and Johnson, Dale D. *Teaching Reading Comprehension.* New York: Holt, Rinehart and Winston, 1978.

Smith, Frank. *Understanding Reading: A Psycholinguistic Analysis of Reading and Learning to Read.* New York: Holt, Rinehart and Winston, 1978.

Learning to Read
through Literature

C. Ann Terry
University of Houston

Reading instruction is most effective when children are allowed and encouraged to learn by actually reading books.

Reading books aloud, using books as springboards to other activities, and encouraging children to read independently are components of an instructional program that emphasizes wide reading and exposure to books.

What is the primary function of a reading teacher? Pretend you are answering this question as part of a survey and select one of the following:

1. to ensure that children are competent users of word analysis strategies
2. to offer a program in which comprehension skills are mastered
3. to provide children with many opportunities to read books
4. to teach children to read for information and to solve problems

If you think that the acquisition of skills is most important in learning to read, you probably chose numbers 1 or 2; however, if you believe that children learn to read by reading, you more than likely selected item number 3. In a similar survey, thirty reading teachers were asked to respond to the same question. Given the same four choices, none of the teachers in the sample chose item number 3 as being the most important function of a reading teacher.

Yet, according to many recognized authorities in reading today, "children learn to read only by reading" (Smith, 1973, p. 195) and instruction can not and should not occur separately from reading books. In essence, teaching reading skills in isolation, apart from books, is like teaching children to swim while out of the water.

This viewpoint is substantiated by significant research. Bamberger (1976, p. 61), in an attempt to discover why some children read and others do not, studied a variety of reading situations. An examination of the results showed clearly that the exceptional classes where the children read well and extensively were not those in which the teacher concentrated on reading skills. Rather, they were classes in which the main object was to develop joy in reading through acquaintance with books from the very beginning of reading instruction. Bamberger concluded (p. 63): "Education in reading used to have the book as its goal; today the book is more than a goal, it is the means to an end."

Findings from another significant study (Durkin, 1966) suggest that children who learn to read early have been read to frequently. A parent or an older child has answered their questions concerning the material read. The children involved in Durkin's study frequently saw adults reading, and reading was considered a pleasurable activity in their homes. Larrick (1975, p. 15) summarizes the implications of this research: "The two important ways to cultivate a child's readiness for reading are (1) to develop each child's aptitude for reading through rich experience with oral language and (2) to create eagerness to read through continuing pleasure in books."

If a teacher believes that children learn to read through contact with literature, how can an instructional program be planned that emphasizes wide reading and exposure to books? One successful method is to organize a literature-based reading program, which can be described as having three basic components: (1) reading books aloud; (2) using books as springboards to a variety of writing, reading, listening, and language experiences; and (3) encouraging children to read independently.

Reading Books Aloud. Research has shown that throughout the elementary grades, children profit from hearing books read aloud. For example, Cohen (1968) found that second graders who were identified as slow readers benefited from a year-long read-aloud program. Teachers read stories to children and then engaged them in a variety of activities such as dramatizations, book discussions, and art projects. At the end of the year, work knowledge, quality of vocabulary, and reading comprehension of the children in the experimental classes increased significantly over the control group classes. Here are some suggestions for teachers who are planning a read-aloud program:

Establish a specific time each day for reading books or poems aloud.

Try to select books or poems that will be interesting to both boys and girls.

When choosing books to read aloud, consider the language of the story. Is is creative and enjoyable to hear? Is the book well written? Does the story flow smoothly for reading aloud?

If the reading is for younger children, consider the size and quality of the illustrations when selecting books.

If a book lends itself to discussion, make time to talk about it. Conversations about books help children develop and clarify concepts, broaden their experience, and extend their knowledge of words.

Using Books as Springboards. Books can be used to initiate a variety of arts experiences that will contribute to children's growth in reading. For example, dramatic activities inspired by books such as *Sam* or *Alexander and the Terrible, Horrible, No Good, Very Bad Day* are enjoyable and offer children beneficial language and reading experiences. Both of these stories provide excellent material for role playing in the classroom. Books can also motivate children to write—and read and share their creative products. Wordless books, such as the *Alligator's Toothache, Ah-Choo*, or *A Birthday Wish*, provide opportunities for children to write and then read their own texts. Older students might write and share continuing episodes for books such as *Julie of the Wolves, Island of the Blue Dolphins, Call It Courage, A Wrinkle in Time*, or *Sing Down the Moon.* Books can also initiate listening experiences. For example, children can record familiar folktales on cassette tape. *The Three Bears* might be retold from Goldilocks's point of view or *The Three Billy Goats Gruff* might become a modernized twentieth century tale recorded on cassette tape for other students in the class to hear.

Encouraging Independent Reading. If children are to read widely, many different kinds of books should be available within the classroom. In addition to a variety of books, special children's periodicals such as *Cricket* and *National Geographic World* are a valuable part of the classroom collection. Also, new books and materials should be added to the classroom collection as frequently as possible. It is important to talk about the new materials because children often show an interest in reading books that the teacher introduces or discusses with them.

It is a good idea to set aside a special time each day for students to read the variety of material that is available. This is especially important because children may not actually read at any other time during the day. Many teachers select thirty minutes before or after lunch, or use a period of time near the end of the school day when everyone can read without interruption—including the teacher.

If at all possible, provide a comfortable place for children to read. A rug, soft pillows, or an old sofa can change a formal reading setting into a warm, cozy one where pleasurable reading is likely to occur. The classroom environment communicates to the young readers that reading is an activity that is to be explored, enjoyed, and shared.

If children are to learn to read through literature, as this article suggests, teachers of reading should continue to find ways of making books an integral part of the instructional program. Then, and only then, can books become the means to a desirable end for children who are becoming readers.

References

Bamberger, Richard. "Literature and Development in Reading." In *New Horizons in Reading.* Newark, Del.: International Reading Association, 1976.

Cohen, Dorothy H. "The Effect of Literature on Vocabulary and Reading Achievement." *Elementary English* 45 (February 1968): 209-13, 216.

Durkin, Delores. *Children Who Read Early: Two Longitudinal Studies.* New York: Teachers College Press, 1966.

Larrick, Nancy. *A Parent's Guide to Children's Reading,* 4th ed. New York: Bantam Books, 1975.

Smith, Frank. *Psycholinguistics and Reading.* New York: Holt, Rinehart and Winston, 1973.

Additional Resources

Abjørsen, Peter Christian, and Jorgan, Moe F. *The Three Billy Goats Gruff,* illustrated by Marcia Brown. New York: Harcourt, 1957.

Biorst, Judith. *Alexander and the Terrible, Horrible, No Good, Very Bad Day.* Paterson, N.J.: Atheneum, 1972.

DeGroat, Diane. *Alligator's Toothache.* New York: Crown, 1977.

Emberly, Ed. *A Birthday Wish.* Boston: Little, Brown, 1977.

Galdone, Paul. *The Three Bears.* New York: Seabury, 1972.

George, Jean. *Julie of the Wolves,* illustrated by John Schoenherr. New York: Harper and Row, 1972.

L'Engle, Madeleine. *A Wrinkle in Time.* New York: Farrar, Straus, 1962.

Mayer, Mercer. *Ah-Choo.* New York: Dial Press, 1976.

O'Dell, Scott. *Island of the Blue Dolphins.* Boston: Houghton Mifflin, 1960.

O'Dell, Scott. *Sing Down the Moon.* New York: Dell, 1973.

Scott, Ann Herbert. *Sam,* illustrated by Symeon Shimin. New York: McGraw-Hill, 1967.

Sperry, Armstrong. *Call It Courage.* New York: Macmillan, 1940.

Periodicals

Cricket Magazine. Open Court Publishing Company, LaSalle, Ill.

National Geographic World, National Geographic Society, Washington, D.C.

III Evaluation in Language Education

Doris Gunderson, editor
U. S. Office of Education

Introduction

Those who work in various areas of language arts education are caught between two opposing and sometimes mutually exclusive trends: the pressure for accountability and its attendant testing which sometimes runs counter to the recommendations of specialists in learning theory and language education for a more humanistic approach. Researchers in language arts have much to do. Tests in various areas of the language arts, particularly in listening, speaking, and language development, may not be accurate enough to reveal differences in the best-designed experimental studies of methodology or procedure. We do not even have a clear picture of the basic development of some language skills. In language arts evaluation and research, some major questions emerge: (1) How can we measure or assess how well children are developing their speaking, reading, and writing abilities? (2) How can we evaluate the effectiveness of language arts education programs? and (3) How can we learn more about how children develop speaking, reading, and writing abilities? These questions are interrelated as practitioners and researchers work in separate ways to gather information about children's language. The articles in this section explore some ways in which adults can look at various aspects of language learning in children and they point to some of the issues that face all of us who work with young children.

In the first article, Lilja outlines the essential factors for effective assessment of children's language growth and suggests ways of gathering information on individual students. Saville-Troike explores the wide range of techniques, formal and informal, that are needed by teachers if they are to assess children's understanding of the various aspects of language. She emphasizes evaluation as an integral component of interaction in the classroom. Kolczynski looks at the question of judging the range of children's uses of language and describes two schemes for observing and categorizing these uses. Singleton focuses on the assessment of reading behaviors; Odland explores response to literature as it contributes to language development; and Petty discusses the appraisal of composition abilities. All three writers stress that evaluation is a continuous, ongoing process and that a variety of procedures should be used.

If we are to find more effective ways of assessing children's language growth and development, further research is needed. DeStefano directs attention to the patterned strategies that children employ to discover language systems, and emphasizes the importance of such patterns for research. She outlines areas of current concern for the practitioner as well as the researcher who is interested in the language development of children.

Measuring the Effectiveness of Language Education

Linnea D. Lilja
University of Missouri

Evaluation in the language arts should focus on a wide range of factors related to children's growth as effective communicators.

Listening to and observing children, with a number of questions in mind, can provide the language arts teacher with much valuable information for program planning.

Each child who enters the classroom brings along some personally adequate method of communication. Evolved through trial and error, the system developed until the child could obtain satisfactory responses to expressed demands, to questions asked, and to ideas or emotions. But within the school environment the child comes into a new setting where this communication system may or may not be effective.

Teachers of young children have two concerns: (1) How effective is the child's language usage upon entering the class and when leaving it? and (2) Has language study improved communication capabilities, and if so, how? The following are suggested evaluation factors (no priority implied) for determining the child's effectiveness in understanding and being understood—the objective of good language teaching.

1. *Awareness.* Is the child aware of language as a method of communication, serving definite purposes?

2. *Spontaneous Use.* It is widely accepted that the more secure a child feels in language, the greater the spontaneity of usage. An eager "oh-oh" accompanying hand-raising demonstrates this.

3. *Using Nonverbal Signals or Body Language.* Does the child, responding to questions, employ signals—pointing, walking toward an object, head movements, hand symbols—rather than words to communicate? Evaluating the nonverbal

factor indicates possible starting points for instruction and, subsequently, checks language development and use of the appropriate nonverbal signal. Considering custom, visualize the confusion (temporary, one hopes) when shaking the head vertically is intended to mean "no" and horizontally implies "yes." Experience may correct confusion here, but subtler signals require more specific approaches and actions. A word of caution—interpret the signal correctly. A librarian, reading to a small boy, used different voices for the characters. Before long the boy displayed signals of boredom (squirming, arm-stretching). When the reader closed the book and simply told the story, the youngster listened attentively. While seeming not to hear the story when it was read, he really just had not liked the way it was done.

4. *Baby Talk.* Does the child have obvious "cutesy" speech patterns, either in word choice, word pronunciation, or sentence structure? The key obviously is to allow for (a) developmental differences—preschoolers are more apt to display these language patterns than first graders; (b) excessively long, continued use—a second grader should be beyond this stage.

5. *Dialect or Regional Language Usage.* In a mobile society, dialect or regional usage becomes a more important element of language than many people realize. When a child uses a "different" word to describe something and does not communicate, what then? An adult might search for alternative words or explanation, but a child may be unable to do so. Other dialectical considerations include the form of words (*knit* or *knitted* as past tense), and pronunciations (*cot* and *caught* sound alike), and, while not strictly under this heading, slang usage. Excessive reliance upon so-called current idiom, to the point where communication with others is inhibited, should be noted with the eventual goal of widening the child's language use.

6. *Use of Time-, Place-, and Thought-Holders.* How often has the child used "ya know" in conversation as a substitute for uncertain words or as a subtle asking for help—because you *do* know? What about use of "hm-hm" or "uh-uh" to hold a discussion position while contemplating what to say next? Admittedly, everyone does these things on occasion, so the major consideration is how often and how consistently?

7. *Word Choice.* Does the child obviously possess an ample basic vocabulary to enable smooth, comprehensive expression? Analyzing the kinds of words being used permits easy evaluation of that language component. Consider (a) how many empty words are used in daily speech; (b) does the student know the names of all the objects, activities, emotions, and so on, encountered every day; (c) is there any attempt to use word variety in everyday speech; (d) are the same words monotonously repeated; (e) how often are baby talk and unusual words used instead of familiar, easily understood ones; (f) is there evidence of curiosity to know words and their meanings; (g) are their questions about or experiments with words and sounds; (h) is there experimentation with word forms or word invention? Mistakes can be an alert—a signal that the child is testing the use of language. However, when the youngster is unable to discern errors or overgeneralizations after a reasonable time—for instance, an older child still uses "foots" in place of "feet"—there is reason for concern.

8. *Sentence Patterns.* The first, and most important, of two considerations here is whether the child is able to orally present (a) a total thought (statement that conveys meaning), and (b) in a complete sentence structure where appropriate. It is known that in talking, people often do not express themselves in complete sentences—but in most cases they could do so if required. Similarly, the concern is whether the child can, if necessary, express the thought within a sentence structure. Otherwise this may mean that children must be placed in situations that make such linguistic demands.

The second consideration is whether the child can use a variety of sentence structures, including questions, exclamations, and so on, with variations of word order in simple sentences. Mature speakers typically use more than a simple noun-verb pattern in their speech. Variety of sentence structure may be an indicator of how secure children feel with their language.

9. *Thought Structure.* When all is said and done, what is language but communication of thought? If the child seems unable to structure ideas into clear communication units, then there is inevitable breakdown between speaker and lis-

tener. For easy detection, have the child orally work through a simple problem, noting logical order and language precision. Whether or not language is needed *for* thought, language is a crucial element in *communicating* thought. The child should exhibit the ability to use literal, inferential, and creative levels of thinking.

Ways of Collecting Information

The above list of evaluative factors may seem to be too many ideas to keep in mind when the children are huddled around, all talking at once. But try making a checklist to work through for each child on different days. What is the method of evaluation? Merely listening and taking notes:

1. Listen to a tape recording of a part of the school day.
2. Have an aide listen for specific language patterns.
3. Watch for and note enthusiastic and spontaneous verbal response from the child.
4. Discern the kinds of concepts a child wishes to discuss.
5. Plan discussions with various thought-provoking questions serving as a stimulus. (This can be done within any learning situation—a science lesson, reading a story aloud, and so on. Questions requiring nonfactual answers are, of course, the most effective for encouraging spontaneous, free language usage.)
6. Listen to or record playground language. (How does the child talk to peers? Show-and-tell is not always effective for gathering language information because the situation is more formal, involving a greater number of children.)

Take language samples from differing groups: one-to-one, small, and large, with both familiar and unacquainted people. Various settings and responses are vital to an effective evaluation.

Well-rounded, well-planned, well-organized language programs will encourage children who are secure in their use of language, unafraid of telling what they know to a group, and aware of the basic power and persuasiveness of the words they use. Assessment of a wide range of factors in children's growth as communicators can give the feedback educators need to plan and improve such programs.

Discovering What Children Know about Language

Muriel Saville-Troike
Georgetown University

Discovering what children know about language, especially how well they understand the language forms used by teachers and in books, is an essential prerequisite to planning learning experiences for them.

Teachers need a variety of techniques, formal and informal, if they are to assess children's understanding of the various aspects of language, including meaning, phonology, grammar, the speaker's intent, and appropriate social use.

Testing what children know about language can be accomplished as an integral component of the ongoing interaction in the classroom rather than an isolated, unrealistic activity.

The language competence of children is generally evaluated in terms of their ability to perform linguistically—that is, by judging how fluently they speak, and eventually how well they read and write. Because language is the primary medium through which all education takes place, and because the development of productive language skills depends on prior receptive competence, it is even more important for teachers to know how well children understand the language of instruction. We can assume that children who do speak fluently, who do learn to read and write well, and who do master the content areas of instruction are also competent in the skills and processes involved in understanding language; but often children must fail in our educational system before we discover that their language knowledge did not meet the demands of learning in the school situation. Discovering what children know about language, particularly how well they understand and interpret the language forms addressed to them by teachers and books, is essential if teachers are to provide appropriate and adequate opportunities to learn.

Some existing forms of evaluation provide information on children's receptive competence in language, or can be adapted to do so, but teachers need a variety of testing procedures to check on the complex skills and processes involved in understanding English.

Meaning

The most obvious and easily tested area of language is vocabulary. Evaluation procedures commonly involve asking children to identify a picture or object that is named. Not so easy to test, however, are words that refer to abstract concepts or relationships. Understanding of words that express actions and spatial or temporal relations can be checked while playing games that require following directions (for instance, "Skip to the table after you stand on a chair" or "Put the block under the desk and then take the book from Mary"). Perception of humor is also a good indicator of the understanding of meaning. Some nonsense directives may be included, such as "Walk on the ceiling" or "Tiptoe noisily," where laughter will be the appropriate response. Children may also be asked to identify what's funny in a series such as "The dog barked, the cat meowed, the horse quacked" or in sentences such as "He painted a picture with his scissors." At a more advanced level, identifying what's funny about sentences such as "The boy was very bad, but the teacher scolded him" is a good test for ability to understand the conjunctions which indicate logical relationships between parts of a sentence.

Phonology and Grammar

Understanding the meaning of words when they occur in context necessarily requires understanding phonology and grammar as well as vocabulary. By the time they are five or six years old, children seldom have difficulty in perceiving the sounds of the language they have heard spoken around them. Even children who cannot yet produce all of the sounds accurately (saying "wabbit" for *rabbit*, perhaps, or "tink" for *think*) can generally hear the differences between *w* and *r* or *t* and *th* when they are pronounced by others. When children have grown up with a language other than English, or with a variety of English which is different from the teacher's, some misunderstanding of sounds may result.

Generally, however, except when words are used unnaturally out of context, sounds are not a source of confusion for children who have adequate knowledge of vocabulary and grammar. Depending on the native language or regional variety, potential homophones include such pairs as *cot* and *caught, witch* and *which, share* and *chair,* or *day* and *they,* but using such words in context will automatically make their meaning clear. Testing for perception of such sound distinctions is probably important only to identify possible causes of spelling errors, and thus it is of minimal relevance for teachers of young children. They do not in themselves seem to interfere with learning to read.

It is relevant, however, to test children who do not pronounce plural or past tense endings (saying "dog" for *dogs* and "talk" for *talked*) for their understanding of the grammatical concepts of number and tense. Not pronouncing the final sounds does not indicate that the grammatical concepts are missing. The omission of *s* or *ed* is quite common in some varieties of spoken English and does not cause problems in communication; however, children are expected to understand such grammatical forms by the time they come to school and to perceive the final inflection when it is pronounced by others or occurs at the end of words in writing.

Receptive knowledge about number, tense, and other points of grammar can be tested by asking children to identify which of a pair of spoken sentences correctly describes a picture or situation: "John is walking" or "John walked"; "Mary is cold" or "Mary has a cold"; "It is raining" or "It has rained"; "We have a hamster" or "We have hamsters"; "John is taller than Bill" or "Bill is taller than John." Children may also be asked to identify which picture or object(s) a single sentence is describing: "The cats are playing" (a second picture might be of a single cat playing); "The dog is going to eat" (a second picture might show a dog eating; a third picture, a dog leaving an empty dish); "The girl is bigger than the boy" (a second picture might be of a boy who is bigger than a girl).

Understanding of direct and indirect objects can be tested by placing objects (including perhaps toy animals or dolls) on a table and asking children to follow directions such as: "Give a horse to the doll"; "Give a doll to the horse"; "Give the doll a horse." Children have not yet learned all of the basic grammatical structures of English by the time they come to school. For example, the third sentence ("Give the doll a horse") is normally not understood until a later age. The same is true of understanding passive sentences. In such cases it is important for teachers to be aware of what children cannot developmentally be expected to know about grammar so they will not attempt to teach language form at an inappropriate level.

Intent

It is important to assess understanding of the speaker's intent (pragmatic competence). To function in a classroom, children must understand that the apparent declarative sentence "It's too noisy in here" is not merely a statement of fact, but a request to be quiet, and that "It's too noisy out in the hall" is probably a request for someone near the door to shut it. Children's understanding of the intent of common classroom experiences can be tested by a multiple choice technique: for example, "If I say 'Johnny, would you like to sit down now,' am I *asking* Johnny if he wants to sit down or am I *telling* him to sit down?" Children's understanding may also be tested by asking them to paraphrase or provide a translation: "When I say 'Johnny, would you like to sit down now,' what do I mean?" When "Johnny" answers "no" to such a command when it is used in school, it is important for the teacher to be able to distinguish between impudence and inadequate knowledge of the pragmatic meaning of linguistic forms.

Social Use

A final aspect of language to be tested is the knowledge of appropriate structures or rules for the use of language in various social contexts (sociolinguistic competence). Examples of misunderstanding can be informally observed: the little girl who has just learned to raise her hand when she wants to talk, raises her hand to join a conversation with peers on the playground; or a child calls the teacher or principal (a family friend) by their first name. A systematic evaluation of this dimension of understanding is desirable.

Both the testing and teaching of socially appropriate language use can be accomplished by constructing role playing situations, with children taking different roles (parent, child, teacher, nurse, baby) in different suggested settings (inside the classroom, on the playground, at the dinner table). In such hypothetical situations, a purpose for the communication should also be specified, such as comforting someone who is hurt, requesting a toy or second cookie, or apologizing or making an excuse for breaking something. Teachers may also participate in different roles and make calculated mistakes in sociolinguistic behavior, asking children to identify what the teacher did wrong. Children should never be asked to correct one another unless it is clear that the mistakes are intentional.

Ways of Looking at Language Use

Richard G. Kolczynski
Ball State University

Almost all speech acts are meant to communicate or serve a social function.

Children must learn to use language for a wide range of social functions.

Observing and categorizing children's language can help adults understand the communicative process and provide situations which help children expand their use of language.

Language is a system by which speakers interact with each other in order to communicate. Most of our speech acts have a social purpose, to which we as adults must become sensitive. For communication to be meaningful and shared, we not only need to be aware of the actual words and expressions (linguistic form) of a spoken message, but also the social function of what is said.

It is important to realize that the message may have more than one purpose or function. For example, "Children at Play" is a familiar sign found near schools and playgrounds. The sign, although written instead of spoken, not only serves as an announcement or statement, but as a warning to drivers of moving vehicles. In oral language, "good morning" may be a greeting, an invitation to discuss the weather, or a cue to begin a conversation about almost anything. Sometimes we ask a question, such as "What did the midget say to the giraffe?", but we actually do not expect our listener to answer the question. As in most jokes, "I don't know" serves as a signal for the speaker's "punch-line," rather than as an admission of ignorance. The form of what is said, therefore, does not always match its function. Adults should familiarize themselves with the variety of meanings that children are able to express through the use of language (Tough, 1976, p. 76).

A number of checklists and systems have been developed to assist teachers in observing, recording, and appraising language behavior in classrooms. Simon and Boyer (1967, 1970) have compiled an anthology of ninety-two different systems. Some of these systems help us observe the proportion of teacher-versus-student talking in the classroom. Others aim at describing the way in which children use language for social purposes. Research on language use has produced several systems for classifying the functions of language. Two of them—by Halliday (1975) and Tough (1976)—are discussed below and they provide a useful outline to help parents and teachers look at children's use of language.

Halliday's Scheme

Observing how children use language can provide insights into the communicative nature of language: conveying a message and fulfilling a purpose. Halliday's studies of children's language led him to conclude that language development is a process of acquiring "meaning potential." As children experience language and its many uses, they gradually "learn how to mean." Halliday is concerned with how children communicate meaning to others; intention and use are most important in understanding how language conveys meaning. He argues that the "child's awareness of language cannot be isolated from [the child's] awareness of language function"; any attempt to analyze the language used in communication must include consideration of form and function. That is, the actual words used in speech must be related to the speaker's purposes and to the context in which talking takes place.

Halliday's system for classifying language includes seven categories of language function, which define language according to its uses and the intentions of the child.

1. Instrumental. Used to get something the child wants, to satisfy needs or desires, to get things done. Examples: "I want," "I need."

2. Regulatory. Used to control the behavior of others; directed toward a particular individual. Examples: "Do this," "Bring me."

3. Interactional. Used to establish and define social relationships. Examples: "Hello," "Pleased to see you."

4. Personal. Used to express one's individuality and personality; to express feelings. Examples: "Here I come," "I don't like it."

5. Heuristic. Used to explore the environment, to acquire knowledge and understanding. Examples: "What is it called?" "I wonder why?"

6. Imaginative. Used to create an environment of one's own, to express fantasy, in poetry and imaginative writing. Examples: "Let's pretend," writing or telling "tall tales."

7. Informative. Used to communicate information to someone who does not already possess that information. Examples: "I've got something to tell you," "I've got to report."

Most of our everyday language probably can be categorized as instrumental or interactional. The language found in school serves a heuristic or "find out" function when emphasis is placed on "knowing" through language. At home and in their neighborhoods, children ask questions about their world—the heuristic function of language. Going to school introduces children to the more formal aspects of questioning and searching for answers while continuing to foster natural exploratory behavior.

Much of what takes place in schools requires informative uses of language. It is through this function that information is communicated to someone who does not already possess it. Students need chances to practice this function through helping and "telling" each other. A student's ability to impart or share knowledge is often the basis for educational evaluation. Halliday insists, however, that experiences with the full range of language functions are necessary for developing language as a means of communication.

Tough's System

A very practical and manageable classification system for the uses of language was developed by Joan Tough (1976), specifically for teachers who want to appraise children's use of language during classroom activities. Tough's classification scheme includes seven uses of language, with corresponding strategies that serve each category and reveal the child's reason for talking.

Tough states that "In making an appraisal of the child's use of language, it is the content of the child's talk, the kind of information with which [the child] deals, and the manner in which [the child] deals with it, that is important" (p. 86). Tough recommends the use of tape recorders to collect examples of children's talk, from which transcriptions of part or all of the sample may be made. Using pictures and picture books to stimulate discussion allows the teacher to develop skill in conversing with children, recording their conversation, questioning them in order to extend

Classified Uses of Language
(Adapted from Joan Tough, *Listening to Children Talking*,
pp. 78–80.)

Uses	Strategies
Self-maintaining the rights and property of the self.	Referring to physical and psychological needs and wants. Protecting the self and self interests. Justifying behavior or claims. Criticizing or threatening others.
Directing the child's own activity and that of others.	Monitoring one's own actions. Directing the actions of the self and others. Collaborating with others.
Reporting on present and past experience.	Labelling the components of the scene. Referring to detail, incidents, sequence of events. Making comparisons; recognizing related aspects. Analysis of the above features. Extracting, recognizing the central meaning. Reflecting on the meaning of experiences or feelings.
Logical reasoning.	Explaining a process. Recognizing causal, dependent relationships. Recognizing problems, solutions. Justifying actions, judgments. Reflecting on events and drawing conclusions. Recognizing principles.
Predicting and anticipating possibilities.	Anticipating, forecasting events. Anticipating the detail of events, sequence of events, problems and solutions, courses of action. Predicting the consequences of actions or events.
Projecting into the experiences of others.	Projecting into: the experiences of others, the feelings of others, the reactions of others, situations never experienced.
Imagining a scene for play through talk.	Developing an imaginary situation based on real life or on fantasy. Developing an original story.

their observations and to reveal their capabilities, and appraising their use of language.

Note-taking and record-keeping of what each child does with language provide the basis for planning classroom activities that promote skills of communication. Tough explains that parents and teachers need to provide a wide variety of experiences during which children use language for different purposes. By keeping careful notes on children's use of language, teachers will have a continuous record of "evidence of what the child can do with language at particular points and in particular situations" (Tough, p. 109). Such records will guide teachers in promoting appropriate and effective uses of language during classroom activities. Too often the natural, warm, and personal talk found in conversations at home is ignored in task-oriented classrooms where emphasis is placed on what Halliday would call informative uses of language. As Pinnell (1975, p. 326) suggests, teachers need to "examine their own behavior and become aware of how they interact with others. They need opportunities to listen to themselves and to children talking and to look at the meanings and intentions behind the way they use language."

Implications

While the above classification systems may prove useful in organizing our thoughts about how language is used, we must realize that they are only categorizations. They will not always fit the real world (Criper and Davies, 1977, p. 173). Also, the functions of language are not discrete. Any single speech act can serve many functions at the same time. What is important for adults to understand is that there are many ways to communicate, causing varying degrees of difficulty in arriving at shared understanding. We must be aware of the principles of what we say, how we say it, and what we mean as they come together in a social context. The ultimate goal of language education, whether at home or at school, should be to open the way for greater and more effective use of language that is appropriate to given social situations.

References

Criper, Clive, and Davies, Alan. "Research on Spoken Language in the Primary School." In *Language and Learning in Early Childhood*, edited by Alan Davies, pp. 143–86. London: Social Science Research Council, 1977.

DeStefano, Johanna S. "Register: Social Variation in Language Use." *Elementary School Journal* 72 (January 1972): 189-94.

Halliday, M. A. K. *Learning How to Mean—Explorations in the Development of Language.* London: Edward Arnold, 1975.

Pinnell, Gay Su. "Language in Primary Classrooms." *Theory into Practice* 14 (December 1975): 318-27.

Simon, A., and Boyer, E. G. *Mirrors for Behavior: An Anthology of Classroom Observation Instruments*, vols. 1-6. Philadelphia: Research for Better Schools, 1967.

Simon, A., and Boyer, E. G. "Mirrors for Behavior." In *Classroom Interaction Newsletter*, special edition, 2 vols. Philadelphia: Research for Better Schools, 1970.

Tough, Joan. *Listening to Children Talking.* London: Schools Council Publications, 1976.

Evaluating Some Early Reading Behaviors

Carlton M. Singleton
Educational Consultant

Different circumstances surround the acts of learning to speak and learning to read; motivation is the key.

Measurement of a child's attitude toward reading is essential in helping children learn to read.

A steady and continuous evaluation plan, focusing on various aspects of the reading process, is a vital part of teaching children to read.

Children should learn to read as easily as they learn to speak. Both tasks require similar intellectual capacity and concentrated effort. Yet every normal child learns to speak easily, but not every child learns to read easily. Why should this be so? What are the differences between learning to speak and learning to read? What role can evaluation play in helping young children learn to read and speak with equal ease?

There are many differences in the circumstances under which children learn to speak and learn to read:

Young children learn to speak in an environment in which everyone speaks. Not everyone in the environment reads.

A child learns to speak in a home-centered environment which is part of the child's life every waking moment. The school environment surrounds the child only part of some days.

Learning to speak means moving at one's own pace and at times one's own choosing. Learning to read means adjusting to someone else's pace and choice of time.

Young children get a great deal of pleasure from their attempts to learn to speak. In the beginning, every word is greeted with praise. They soon learn that speech is the major avenue for satisfying needs and wants. Learning to read, on the other hand, usually offers little in the way of immediate satisfaction.

Considering the major differences in circumstances, it is apparent that motivation to learn to speak is overwhelming, and motivation to learn to read may be almost nonexistent in many children's situations.

Children come to school from many different home environments and a variety of socioeconomic levels, and they are the issue of parents from varying educational strata. In some homes there are many, often used, reading materials; in others there are none. For some children, being read to is an everyday and very pleasurable experience. For other children, the television set is the only channel to things outside the immediate here and now. The child who is read to understands the pleasure that books can bring. The child who is never read to may well consider books as unnecessary or irrelevant. Certainly there is a difference in attitude toward reading on the part of children from such widely differing backgrounds.

The measurement of a child's attitude toward reading is a prime essential in helping children learn to read. Yet, despite the plethora of tests available to check a child's progress in reading, there are few instruments designed to determine a child's interest in reading. Luckily, the wise teacher and the interested parent can easily determine a child's attitude toward reading for themselves. Attitude is so important that these questions should be asked, and answered affirmatively, before formal reading instruction is begun:

> Does the child enjoy the stories in books? Like having them read aloud?
>
> Does the child want to handle the books which have been read? Want to hold them and look at the pictures?
>
> Does the child want favorite stories read again? Attempt to "read" them by reciting the story while turning the pages?
>
> Does the child listen attentively while being read to? Sometimes listen with closed eyes as though imagining the story? Has the child ever drawn a picture to illustrate a story?
>
> Does the child understand what you are doing when you look in a book for the answer to a question that has been asked? Has the child ever suggested that you "look it up in a book"?
>
> Does the child understand what you are doing when you follow a recipe in a book? Or follow any directions for doing something?

An answer of "yes" to some or most of the above questions is an indication of a healthy attitude toward reading. Children thus motivated are generally enthusiastic about reading, and that enthusiasm should continue.

Early attitudes are not a guarantee, however. In learning to read, motivation plays such an important part in the day-to-day progress that the child's attitude toward reading should be constantly and carefully watched. The above questions should be regularly considered, and any waning of interest evidenced by a change in answers should be noted as a warning sign.

Children learn at their own pace and in their own time. Too rapid a pace or too much pressure at the wrong time can easily cause interest to slacken and the child's attitude toward reading to change. The pace at which a child learns to read should be constantly checked by ongoing evaluation. There are several aspects of reading behavior which can easily be checked by observing children and asking them questions.

Among other things, learning to read means learning the code by which written English represents spoken English. Since the child learning to read already knows and understands spoken English, he or she must learn to link that spoken English with its written form. To do this the child must learn the letters of the alphabet, the sounds used in spoken English, and the relationships between the two. A young reader must learn to hear the separate sounds in spoken English in order to be able to recognize that the words *ball*, *bat*, and *belt* start with the same sound, as do the words *cat*, *kick*, and *Christmas*. In the first example, the child learns that the sound heard first in the word *ball* is indicated by the letter *b*, and in the second example the sound heard first is indicated by the letter *c*, or *k*, or *ch*. Hearing these separate sounds in words is called auditory discrimination. Lack of auditory discrimination is a common cause for lack of growth in reading. An informal diagnostic inventory must be an ongoing part of the teaching plan to make certain that the learner's growth is steady and sustained.

Evaluation must not be considered as a once-a-month or once-a-year part of learning to read. Many specific reading behaviors are subject to inventory. A steady and continuing evaluation plan covering specific reading skills and behaviors is essential to make certain that each child is learning what the teacher is attempting to teach. The mechanics of reading skills, letter names, auditory discrimination, the functions of punctuation, structural clues, and so on, are well known and subject to specific diagnosis by easily developed teacher questions.

Learning to read means learning to derive meaning directly from the printed word. Certain words in English occur with such high frequency that there are about one hundred that account for about one-half of all words used in written English. Those words are the prepositions, conjunctions, articles, verb auxiliaries, and some adverbs that control the interrelationships of the meaning-filled words in sentences. Another common problem of children who have difficulty in learning to read is caused by skipping over or miscalling these little words. Such problems can handicap children in trying to find meaning in the whole sentence. Determining the child's rate of growth in his mastery of the little words is subject to one hundred percent inventory evaluation. It is not at all difficult to arrange for and maintain a record of pupil masteries over this short list of words.

Evaluation does play an important part in the process of guiding children to growth in reading. A continuing measure of the child's attitude toward reading and a continuing measure of each pupil's mastery of the basic skills of reading can be used to ensure that learning progresses steadily and at the child's own pace. These measures are not formal ones, and they need not take place all at once; they are simple question-and-answer checklists that any teacher can develop and use regularly.

Observing Response to Literature: A Contributor to Language Development

Norine Odland
University of Minnesota

Children respond to the meaning, language, and illustrations they find in carefully selected children's literature. Through those responses they develop greater awareness of language.

By carefully observing and fostering children's responses, a sensitive adult can assess the quality of their experience and provide further opportunities for response.

Response to literature is a natural contributor to a child's language development. Listening to a story or poem provides the stimulus for a child to respond in a variety of ways. Response may be expressed in dramatic play, for example, by pretending to be Goldilocks after hearing "The Three Bears," or in art, as when children draw characters or scenes that have impressed them. There are various potential response modes, but the most frequent responses are those which employ language; and far more oral than written responses come from young children.

Response to literature as a stimulus to language development in young children can be examined in both informal and formal situations. The informal responses are more frequent in the experience of young children; they also are more difficult to define and describe because of the very nature of informality.

In the home environment, when a story is told or read to a child, talking is likely to occur before reading as well as during the story and after it has been read. Sometimes the response may be simply, "read it again"—a positive reaction. The response may be delayed, as it was when a child, aged four, waited impatiently in the grocery check-out line and watched rain clouds coming closer. In an urgent, clear voice she stunned the employees and other shoppers with "We're going to have some weather. It's a-comin'. She's gonna blow" (from *Time of Wonder*, Robert McCloskey, Viking, 1957, p. 32).

Vocabulary is expanded through listening to literature and children's responses reveal the power of vivid words. The book *Bruno Munari's ABC* (Bruno Munari, Collins-World, 1960) gives children a chance to try out new words, especially when they have been encouraged to read along once or twice through the book. The "vertical violet violin" in Munari's book appeals to children because of its rhythm, color, and unusualness. Children repeat such phrases and expand the meaning of the language.

In informal settings, at home or at school, it is important to present literature in a way that encourages children to talk about what they have read or heard. There is need for maintaining a balance between the quiet time for listening or reading and time for talking as a part of enjoying literature. No prescription is effective in constructing such a balance, but a sensitive adult can determine when the balance exists.

In more formal or structured situations, language development is reasonably one of the goals of presenting literature for response. A major goal is enjoyment of literature, and part of that enjoyment is related to appreciation of the language of literature. Effective teaching requires that each child feels confident in being able to respond without relying on the responses of others. Simultaneously, each child respects the responses of other children. As these goals are achieved, there is concurrent development in powers of language, oral and written.

Volume and quantity of response cannot be the sole measure of success. Quality and appropriateness of response are equally significant in children's responses. After a group of children heard McDermott's *The Stonecutter* (Gerald McDermott, Viking, 1975) there was complete silence for more than sixty seconds. A quiet but deliberate voice spoke up, "Pretty soon he will be whittled down to a little bit of nothing." After that, responses came from several children, each listening to the other and each developing ideas about the meaning of the story. Thus, language was used effectively for expressing ideas, not merely for answering questions asked by the teacher.

The adult who seeks to encourage children's language development through response to literature will consider both the selection of materials to be used and the manner in which the literature is presented to young children. If there is to be active, genuine response, children's interests must be considered in choosing stories and poems and there is much within the realm of literature that will appeal to them. After satisfying the criterion of interest, choices can include selections that are also examples of the best literary and artistic quality. Children need models that are worthy of imitation. Although formal study of literature may be inappropriate for young children, exposure to rhythmic flow of language, vivid, concise vocabulary, and writing that is rich in metaphoric language builds background for the young child, who later will use literary devices such as metaphor with appreciation and understanding.

Reading aloud is a good way to discover whether a piece of literature meets the need for excellence in language. The adult who selects stories and poems for children's appreciation, and especially for response to language, will find oral reading a helpful technique in assessment. Further, skill and artistry in oral reading are prerequisites for the person who presents literature to children. Fine language can be demolished by clumsy, flat, oral renditions.

In responding to literature, young children often respond to the illustrations also. The richness of artistic expression in children's literature today encourages such response to visual arts. Talking about a picture may center on clues that are revealed in the drawings, clues to solve a puzzle or to tell what the book is about. Expressing reactions to illustrations that enhance and extend a story results in development of artistic appreciation.

Many so-called wordless books, with little or no text, offer opportunities for eliciting responses, both written and oral, as children tell the story that the pictures represent to them. A child's version of a text for a wordless book can be recorded on tape, and comparisons of versions told by several children provide further genuine reason for discussion based on listening to the versions of the story.

The potential for language development through response to literature can be realized with wise use of the approaches to literature selected by an adult. Assuming that selection has been done with care, the teacher proceeds with methods that encourage response. Prescriptive methods for presenting literature to children are self-defeating. Generally, the teacher will find little use for "right answer" or "yes and no" questions. Minimizing the value of teacher talk and maximizing the value of student talk will go further to ensure that each child has an opportunity to use and expand the power of language.

Little research has been conducted on the subject of young children's response to literature. Even less research has focused directly on the relationship between response to literature and language development. Some evidence indicates that reading to children has a positive influence on their ability to read and to use oral language. Current developments in research are examining the effects of literature on children's language.

Literature offers to children examples of fine use of language. Even if exposed to only a small portion of the body of literature that appeals to children, the young child can be saturated with language from the past and present. Whether exposure is through listening or through reading silently, the possibilities for language development are fully realized when the child has used language to express reactions to what has been heard or read. Response to literature is one way, an important way, for young children to develop their language power.

Assessing Children's Understanding of Composition

Walter Petty
SUNY at Buffalo

The foundations of composition are established even before children learn to write for themselves. Through questioning and other informal techniques, teachers can evaluate the extent to which young children are aware of the fundamentals of good composition.

Evaluation should be an integral part of the whole teaching-learning process, thus enabling the teacher to determine what the child knows about composition and what still needs to be learned.

Children should begin to learn about the composition process in their first school experiences, in kindergarten or possibly in the nursery school. This early learning is subject to evaluation by teacher and parents alike, and leads to an understanding of the fundamentals of composition in relation to children.

The teacher who tells stories to young children is teaching composition, whether it is consciously intended or not. Children catch on rather quickly to the fact that a good story has an interesting beginning, is orderly in development, and has a point or climax. Of course, many children develop such awareness through home experiences. They know the order of events in many stories; they know what the climax is; they even know if words are changed. When the teacher tells about a personal experience, the children again catch on to the importance of sequence and to clarity in what is said. They soon learn that telling something effectively requires consideration of the audience—their interests and experiences—as reflected in the attention shown to the one doing the telling.

While children soon develop a sense of all of these elements, composition teaching really begins as a teacher informally calls attention to the various composition factors. A teacher interested in evaluating children's understanding of these fundamentals of good composition can easily determine the extent to which the children have learned. Certainly this evaluation is not formal, not a testing as we usually think of it—and it should not distract from the major purpose of the storytelling or other communicative act. However, questions such as "What happened next in the story?" lead smoothly to "Why did the author tell that next?"; and "What was it that I said we did on returning from our trip?" may be followed by "Why did I tell that last?" Even "Was there any part of the story that you didn't understand?" need not be separated from "How could that have been told so that you would understand it easily?"

A bit later the teacher can record children's experiences as they tell about them, individually or in a group activity. Again, in the process of recording, the teacher may present a number of the basics of composition to the children—having them state a good beginning sentence, guiding their ordering of sentences, and helping them achieve clarity in these sentences and appeal and accuracy in the words and phrases they use. The importance of the audience who may read what is being composed can receive attention. When appropriate, teachers and students may even talk about such things as margins, capitalization, and punctuation.

The presenting or teaching may be done by calling children's attention to the principles, but it can best be done through an evaluative process—that is, by asking the children questions similar to those suggested above. The object of such questioning is to elicit responses that show the extent of understanding that has been achieved. The process puts learning and evaluation in concert, exercising a basic teaching principle: Evaluation should always be done to determine what has been learned and what still needs to be learned.

When children develop the ability to write stories and other compositions themselves, the learning about composition continues—and for most children becomes more meaningful. A teacher's empathy with the children, combined with the children's desire to do well in the new activity, facilitates learning. If early awareness of composition has been fostered a teacher's task is greatly reduced. That is particularly true if preliminary activities have included rereading what has been written to be sure the message is clear. If the foundation is less than expected or desired, the same approach as recommended for younger children should be used. Also, such activities as arranging pictures in the order of a story; putting objects into classifications according to size, color, and so on; displaying and telling about an object to classmates; telling about one thing that happened or that they saw;

and telling how to do something—to play a game, for instance—are useful in building a foundation for the composition process. However, the most effective activities are those that involve words and sentences, activities that have a communication-by-language purpose.

It is well to keep in mind that composition is a reflection of thinking. Although children may have problems with the motor aspects of writing—and skills such as spelling—or are shy, overactive, or have some other difficulty in oral composition, the evaluation of a child's compositional ability is essentially an evaluation of his or her ability to think and to represent that thinking. The child who can make a complete and to-the-point oral statement shows that thinking is taking place clearly and effectively. That kind of thinking should also be reflected in written composition. Contrarily, the child who voices or writes a garbled statement may be confused or lack experience in such forms of communication. Of course, garbling may be the result of talking or writing without much knowledge of the subject—but a principle of composition is to be knowledgeable about the subject. Teachers obviously can encourage children to talk and write about things within their experience that they know about, and discourage composition subjects that are beyond the range of children's knowledge. This may seem so obvious that it need not be written, but the evidence is rather strong that many teachers assign both written composition topics and oral report subjects about which the children have little knowledge (and often no interest).

Clarity in thinking is clearly related to the unique abilities and experiences of each child. While native ability may be a factor, not all highly intelligent individuals are composers, a fact that suggests that teachers can effectively improve composition by helping children extend and clarify their thinking.

Researching Children's Language

Johanna S. DeStefano
Ohio State University

Language develops in a pattern. The systems children are developing, and the way in which they develop them, also contain patterns.

Researchers need to search out the patterns that are to be learned and the strategies children employ to learn them.

As you can tell from the earlier sections of this book, we now know quite a bit about children's language development. We know, for example, that language develops in a pattern, in stages which each child may go through at slightly different times from other children. And we have come to recognize the active role each child plays in its development. We also know many of the details of the development of sound and grammatical systems of language.

So what don't we know? Or, to put it another way, what else can we learn about how a child develops the entire language system, which includes not only form (such as sound and grammar) but also patterns of use? First, we still have much to learn about how children develop the meaning system of their language. Linguists call this the semantic system. So a major question that's being asked by researchers is how do children learn to mean? How do they actually "make" language convey the meaning they want it to? M.A.K. Halliday, a British language researcher, has been asking this question recently and has turned to a study of how language functions for children (see Halliday, 1975, Part II, for a description of this research). He and other researchers such as Joan Tough (1973) in Britain and Gay Pinnell (1975) in the United States have found that children do learn to vary the way they talk depending on the function they have in mind. However, we still need to clarify the definitions of the various functions and continue to do research on how older children can become

130

even more effective controllers of these functions. We also need to know what home and school environments encourage very important language functions such as language for knowing or for inquiry, and language for self-expression. This latter is of special interest to parents and teachers, both of whom wish to enhance children's control over the language.

Another very exciting research area deals with questions such as how children learn to use their language appropriately, to make their language fit the context they are in. Somehow they learn to carry on a conversation, to engage in classroom talk with teachers, to joke, to talk formally, to use slang—all of the variations that we take for granted. How do they learn those myriad rules we adults know so well about making our language appropriate to the situation? We know, for example, how to talk to an employer, an employee, a friend, a minister, a colleague, a child, and so on. We almost automatically switch our speech to make it appropriate to the listener and to fit the context. Children also have to learn how to do this if they are to be considered native speakers of a language in a particular culture.

Fortunately there are researchers who are asking these questions about how children learn these kinds of rules. It's in its beginning stages, but preliminary results seem to show, again, that children develop their own sets of rules which may or may not match ours. In learning to tell jokes, for example, children's notions of what is funny definitely don't match ours; and what constitutes a joke to them is quite different from adults' ideas of humor (Bauman, 1976).

Most research has emphasized oral language development, especially children's production of oral language; however, many researchers are focusing on research in literacy development—that is, how do children learn to read, spell, and write? That question is crucial in a society where literacy is important and where failure to become literate so evidently abounds. Thus, many of us have turned to studying the process of learning to read, to write, and to spell. Some of the most illuminating research so far has been the work of Charles Read (1975) and, to some extent, Carol Chomsky (1976), on children who have taught themselves to spell. One finds in the literature wonderful messages such as: WUNS A LITL BUNE HOPT A CROS MI LON/AND THAT BUNE HOPT/ RUYT IN MI HAWS AND I HAVE THE/BUNE SUM MILK. [5:2-year-old child (Chomsky, 1976)] or MY WISL IS BROKUN/ DOT MAK NOYS/MY DADAAY WRX HER [5-year-old child (Read, in presentation, 1976)].

Read finds that the self-taught spellers follow patterns. In other words, their spelling is remarkably similar across the entire group and usually very readable. For example, he mentions that the children he studied tended to base their spelling for vowels on the sound of the letter name, and for consonants on that sound minus the vowel sound ("tee" for *t*). So we find in their spelling "fin" for *fine*, "bot" for *boat*, and "fel" for *feel*. When they run out of letter names they often turn to those that contain the sound they're after, so you find "feh" or "fes" for *fish*, where they use either the *s* or *h* in the *sh* sound.

Other findings seem to show that children who have taught themselves to spell have no trouble making the switch to traditional spelling. They seem to understand that the writing system is made up of patterns.

In closing, I would like to stress the discovery of patterns and their importance in the research in children's language development, both oral and written. The systems children are developing are patterned, and the way in which they develop them also contains patterns. It is up to us as researchers to discover both the patterns that are to be learned and the patterned strategies children employ to learn them. Then, we hope, we can aid parents and teachers in helping them match their emerging sets of patterns to those which ultimately will be developed, allowing them to become even more effective users of the language.

References

Bauman, Richard. "The Development of Competence in the Use of Solicitational Routines: Children's Folklore and Informal Learning." *Working Papers in Sociolinguistics* no. 34, May 1976.

Chomsky, Carol. "Invented Spelling in the Open Classroom." In *Child Language—1975*, special edition of *WORD*, edited by Walburga von Raffler-Engel. International Linguistic Association, 1976, 499–518.

Halliday, M.A.K. *Learning How to Mean—Explorations in the Development of Language.* London: Edward Arnold, 1975.

Pinnell, Gay Su. "Language in Primary Classrooms." *Theory into Practice* 14 no. 5 (December 1975): 318–27.

Read, Charles. *Children's Categorization of Speech Sounds in English.* NCTE Research Report #17. Urbana, Ill.: National Council of Teachers of English, 1975.

Tough, Joan. *Focus on Meaning: Talking to Some Purpose with Young Children.* London: George Allen and Unwin, 1973.